ON THE BRINK IN BENGAL

ON THE
BRINK IN
BENGAL

FRANCIS ROLT

PHOTOGRAPHS BY
PETER BARKER

JOHN MURRAY

© Francis Rolt 1991

First published in 1991
by John Murray (Publishers) Ltd
50 Albemarle Street, London W1X 4BD

The moral right of the author has been asserted

British Library Cataloguing in Publication Data
Rolt, Francis, *1955–*
  On the brink in Bengal.
  1. India. North-eastern India. Description and travel
  I. Title
  915.410452

ISBN 0–7195–4907–8

Printed and bound in Great Britain by
Butler & Tanner Ltd
Frome and London

31329. 915.4

To L.R.S.

Contents

Illustrations

The author wishes to thank Peter Barker both for his companionship during the journey and for permission to reproduce the photographs in this book.

Why are jackfruits rough, and mangoes smooth?
Why have boys moustaches, and girls smooth lips?

Santal song

All the people in this book are real.
I have changed their names, and in some cases circumstantial details,
to protect them and their families.

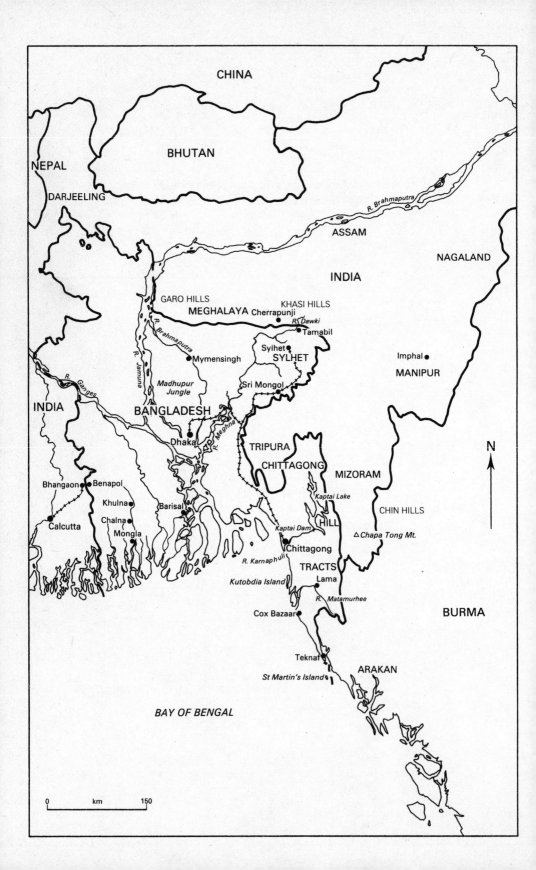

Introduction

The Margin

'Yes, yes we eat cockroaches,' Shanti assured me with a smile, then added, 'fried.'

Her friends reacted with little screams, and clutched each other in delighted disgust at the thought, pulling their filmy pink scarves up over their faces, although it was they who'd encouraged the girl to tell me.

That was twelve years ago, I was twenty-three, little older than the students I was supposedly teaching at Chittagong University. Shanti was a tribal, a Chakma from the Chittagong Hill Tracts.

I didn't know it then, but it wasn't true; none of the many tribal peoples along Bangladesh's northern and eastern borders eat cockroaches, fried or otherwise.

What interests me now is Shanti's complicity in presenting herself and her own people in a bad light to her fellow students – almost without exception Bengali Muslims. She was acting out a role which had been thrust on her – the savage. Unlike other minorities – Hindus, Buddhists or Christians – in Bangladesh she was visibly different from the Muslim majority; her skin was fairer and her features more similar to those of a Burmese, or a Thai than to those of a Bengali; wide, prominent cheekbones and slanting eyes. Her body too was different in that she was evidently fit, used to walking, unlike the majority of other female students who had never walked further than to a rickshaw in their lives. She stood out simply by the way she moved, although she'd learnt to minimize her natural grace. But more important than these things was her friends' almost total ignorance of her way of life and her cultural background. All they knew was that she came from the jungle, so anything was believable.

It seems now that it was this incident, and an attraction to the girl herself, which sparked off a search for information on tribal peoples – made more interesting by their inaccessibility and obscure history, by the lack of written material, and by the rumours and stories. By the time I resigned from the University a year later and moved to the capital, Dhaka, I'd begun to understand something of the dramatic differences between the delta and hill cultures which abut each other, interspersed in places, village by village, for close on a thousand kilometres, from Darjeeling in the eastern Himalayas to where the Bangladesh-Burma border meets the Bay of Bengal at Teknaf.

Bangladesh lies in the northeast corner of the subcontinent, surrounded on three sides by India, and on the fourth by the Bay of Bengal, while in the south it touches Burma. It's a densely populated, largely Muslim country, composed of the great delta system of the Ganges, Meghna and Jamuna rivers. Its people are largely Bengali, they speak an Indo-European language, and on their wet, intensely fertile land they cultivate rice. Despite the traditional conflict between Islam and Hinduism they make up a monolithic, cultural block closely allied to that of Aryan-influenced northern India. To the west of Bangladesh lies the Indian state of West Bengal, whose people are indistinguishable from those of Bangladesh, except as Hindus, and many Bangladeshis still assert that they are, 'Bengalis first and Muslims second'.

To the north and east of this vast riverine flood plain rise the hills and mountains of the Indian tribal states – Assam, Meghalaya ('Abode of the Clouds'), Tripura, Mizoram, Manipur, Nagaland and Arunachal Pradesh – inhabited by many clearly differentiated tribal groups. Historically the tribal nations have had kings and empires, have traded and raided south and east from their jungle fastnesses, and have in places spilt over into the plains. The peoples of this rugged, inaccessible region, which extends from the easternmost range of the Himalayas south as far as Arakan in northern Burma, are Buddhist, Animist, Hindu and Christian, and most of them speak Tibeto-Burmese languages. The nature of the environment they inhabit has militated against uniformity, encouraging the development of extremely localized languages and social systems. Racially, as well as linguistically and culturally, they are closer to the people of southeast Asia than south Asia; their skin is generally pale, their faces tend to be flat, and their eyes slanted – loosely they're described as tribal people.

There's virtually nothing to pull these two groups – Bengalis and tribal peoples – together; the border region, the margin, is a place where two cultural blocks collide, often violently, rather than mix.

It was down this line, through which history has played leapfrog and which delineates one of the clearest ethnic and cultural divisions in the world, that I wanted to travel, following as closely as possible the line of the hills which rise suddenly and dramatically from the delta. No other frontier is comparable in terms of a geographical boundary which marks off one type of people and culture from another; even the great Arab and African cultures are divided by an inhospitable and extensive desert across which travel is slow and difficult. Here two great cultures are thrust into each others' laps, pushed up against each other in a proximity which has led to major wars in the past, and may do so again.

This is more than a contrast between peoples; there is a fundamental conflict of interest brought about by geography, history, culture, language and religion. The line between these two masses, which doesn't exactly follow the international border established with Independence, has great symbolic force, representing the northern and westernmost range of southeast Asian culture, and the easternmost extent of a whole history of subcontinental empires. The ancient Dravidian empire, and those of the Ottoman Turks, the Afghans and the Mughals tried, and failed, to win total control of Bengal's rich rice land and points east. Equally, rulers have driven in from the northeast, from the ancient Ahom empire of Kamrup (Assam), from Cooch Behar, and up from the southeast, from Arakan and from the Chin Hills in Burma. The Portuguese held bits of it briefly, while the British, who did conquer and hold both sides of the line, used a separate set of rules to govern each one.

In learning these things I became aware that the conflict has never been resolved, and in the twentieth century has resulted in incredible stresses and strains on nationhood; nowadays international boundaries and the integrity of the state are held to be inviolable in a way they never were in the past. I became aware of the war which wages between the tribal people and the military in the Chittagong Hill Tracts of Bangladesh, and of the desire for independence still close to the hearts of many Mizo, Naga, Manipuri and other peoples in India's tribal states.

And then I met Bimal.

Komlapur Monastery was only two miles from the house where I lived in Old Dhaka, but the journey took me half an hour by motorbike, for Islampur and Nawabpur roads were blocked with traffic jams of brightly decorated rickshaws, their painted panels depicting idealized village scenes (the cow healthy and fat, the river teeming with fish and every house with a corrugated tin roof), or scenes from films (usually involving a woman dressed daringly in jeans and a bursting T-shirt, and men waving whips or guns).

A tribal boy took me to Bimal's room. Beyond the wide concrete veranda was a square pond surrounded with coconut palms, where children were splashing around, screaming with delight. I asked the boy where he was from, and he answered without emotion, 'Kalampati.'

It seemed better not to ask more, in case it turned out that his family had been among the three hundred tribal people murdered at Kalampati a month previously. This was the reason I wanted to meet Bimal. I was developing the idea of becoming a journalist, and a friend had told me that there was a tribal monk at the monastery who was braver than most, more outspoken and willing to take risks.

News of the massacre at Kalampati was just beginning to leak out – unarmed tribal villagers attacked at night by Bengali Muslim settlers, while the army stood by and watched – and I thought it might be my big break.

Bimal Tishiya Bhikkhu is a member of the Chakma, the largest tribe in the Hill Tracts, and he'd stand out in a crowd even if he didn't shave his head or wear a monk's orange robes, leaving one shoulder bare. His features are strong: prominent cheekbones and brow, and a square jaw, and when he smiles, which is often, his dark eyes are almost forced shut as the muscles tighten.

I blundered into Bimal's room, blurted an introduction and in the same breath asked him about Kalampati. To my surprise he denied any special knowledge of it, other than to repeat what everyone had heard. Poor Bimal, he had no idea why I might be interested in the Hill Tracts or the problems of his people, and had no reason to trust me. He also knew that there were Special Branch officers watching the monastery, to see who came and went, and who spoke to whom; I hadn't taken in the men in dark glasses hanging around in the empty street outside – as out of place as I was, so went away puzzled and disappointed, frustrated in my first journalistic endeavour. But three days later Bimal turned up at the house, saying that he'd like to take English lessons from me. Over the next few months he unwound, and we learnt to trust and confide in each other.

I left Bangladesh in 1980, but somehow kept returning. People say that the first foreign country you work in is like the first love, is the one which takes your heart. I've tried to break my connection with the place several times, but have somehow never managed it, continuing to write about it rather than other, more obviously alluring places where I've lived, such as Nepal.

It was in Nepal, seven years ago, that I met and made friends with the photographer Peter Barker. He was living in a tiny village in the far west, high in the mountains north of Jumla, cut off by snow in winter and surrounded on all sides by spectacular views. He stayed there two years,

4

taking photographs for a book. Since then he's travelled the subcontinent, Tibet and the further reaches of Xinjiang and the Hindu Kush, but never to India's tribal states or to Bangladesh, so he leapt at the idea of joining me. Peter is unflappable and independent – I knew that he wouldn't need looking after. He also seems to be able to nose out interesting people, and the things which can make all the difference between travelling miserably and travelling happily – good food, drink and places to sleep.

Few foreigners have been to the tribal states; the Indian government doesn't issue the requisite Special Permit lightly. Probably I should have known that it wasn't going to work when the First Secretary at the Indian High Commission in London told me that once I'd filled in the forms there'd be no problem. Ushering me out of his office and into the echoing marble hall he said, 'It might take two or three months, but I don't see any reason why Delhi shouldn't give you one.' Four months later I telephoned him. He was most apologetic, 'Oh yes, I've been meaning to get in touch with you, there are some papers from Delhi somewhere on my desk. I can't find them at the moment but I'll send them on to you.' I asked whether the permit had been granted, but he said he couldn't remember, and told me to wait for the papers. They never turned up of course, and when I phoned again he admitted that the government had turned down our request. Personally I doubted whether he'd even bothered to send my application to Delhi, certain that it would be refused.

We had to rein in our plans, but it still wasn't a disaster – the encounter between tribal and Bengali extends in a wide band down both sides of the border. Anyway we thought that we might be able to do some illegal border-hopping from the Bangladesh side once we were in.

The next problem was a Bangladesh visa. Although I've never been deported from Bangladesh – a dubious honour – I have been refused a visa in the past, and a few years ago the country director of Oxfam was refused a visa extension on the grounds that I was a friend of hers. The decision was revoked only under pressure from the British High Commissioner in Dhaka, who'd just given the woman an MBE. As it turned out our visas came through without any difficulty, but it seemed best to fly to Calcutta and cross the land border rather than risk being turned back at Dhaka airport, or finding that I was listed as an undesirable in the large black ledger they leaf through at Immigration. So few outsiders cross by land that I was sure they wouldn't have a copy of that ledger at Benapol, the dusty border post.

After crossing the border into Bangladesh our intention was to go to Dhaka, where I wanted to see Mukta – it was two years since I'd last seen her – and then to travel south, down Bangladesh's leading edge – the seaward side, exposed to the ferocity of cyclones and tidal waves – to Chittagong, perhaps taking in one of the coastal islands. The population of the port city of Chittagong is predominantly Bengali Muslim, but little more than a century ago it was dominated by Arakanese settlers. At the time of the Mughal Emperor Aurangzeb the city had been held by a Portuguese pirate, Bastion Gonsalves, and his half-Arakanese, half-Bengali and Portuguese followers. They had raided as far as Dhaka, ruining and depopulating much of lower Bengal, until Gonsalves was tricked and deprived of his power by the Mughal Governor Shaista Khan. Now, only a few street names remain to remind people of his long reign of terror. From Chittagong we wanted to go further south, to Cox Bazaar, originally another Arakanese town, and then further, as far south as it's possible to go in Bangladesh – to the tiny coral island of St Martins, stuck out in the Bay of Bengal, on the border with Burma.

I hoped that we'd be able to cross the River Naf into Burma itself, into Arakan, and spend some days travelling the northern state, but we decided to leave the issue of Burmese visas until we'd reached Bangladesh.

That itinerary would have taken us as far south as we wanted to go, and from there we intended to head inland, to start following the margin between tribal, or hill and plains cultures. The first stop was to be the forbidden jungles of the Chittagong Hill Tracts, until recently the exclusive preserve of several distinct tribal groups: Chakma, Mru, Marma, Sak, Khyang, Mizo, Tippra and others.

I'd touched the edge of the Hill Tracts before, and had once, as an experiment, asked a boatman on the Kaptai Lake, which marks the area off from the rest of the country, to take me to the far shore, enticingly green. He said that we wouldn't make it, but I told him to try anyway, and paid him in advance. Less than half way across the lake I'd looked back and seen a helicopter rise from a cloud of dust in the army cantonment. It angled across the water towards us, and hovered above the boat, flattening the waves, until the boatman laboriously turned round and started to row us back again. This time I was determined to get into the Hill Tracts, especially as everyone said it was still impossible, and I knew that no one had done it illegally. In the event it proved illogically easy, although three Swedish journalists who tried at about the same time were arrested and deported.

What I didn't know was how much time we'd be able to spend in the Hill Tracts, or how far we'd be able to travel, but I did know that the army was very much in evidence, and that in the last ten years the government had doubled the area's population by flooding it with Bengali Muslim settlers from the poorest parts of Bangladesh – Noakhali and the cyclone-prone islands of the Bay – to such an extent that they now outnumber the tribal people.

Once we'd left the Hill Tracts, assuming we weren't captured and deported, we would go further north and west, to Sylhet, where most of Britain's Bangladeshis come from. The district borders the tribal states of Meghalaya, Tripura and Assam, of which it formed a part until Independence in 1948. All along the fringes of Sylhet lie Khasi and Tippra tribal villages, and the odd megaliths left by the Jaintia people – and then there are the Manipuri, who deny the tag 'tribal', but who came originally from the far northeastern kingdom of Manipur, and are closely related to the Naga of Nagaland, still further north.

After that it was a mystery; I wanted to cross northern Bangladesh, staying as close to the border as possible, but knowing that there are no rivers or roads running east-west, and that the area isn't properly mapped, I wasn't sure whether this would be possible or not. To the west lies the Bangladesh district of Mymensingh, where, amongst the Bengali villages, and in the Madhupur Forest live the Mandi and Mundai tribal groups. We would visit them too I hoped, and then head up the mighty Brahmaputra, fifteen miles wide in places, to Chilmari, to the districts of Rangpur and Dinajpur, to where there are still outposts of the Paharia and the Santal people, who once dominated northern Bengal.

And what did I hope would come out of all this? Two things. First, I wanted to discover the nature of the dividing line between hill and plain, jungle and rice land, tribal and Muslim Bengali. How do their differences manifest themselves? What stresses are placed upon them by the contemporary political reality? By the pressure of population? By economics? By the modern world? And how, if at all, have the people who live on either side of the boundary, sometimes on the wrong side, adapted to, and been influenced by, one another's presence?

Second, I wanted to show Bangladesh for what it is, or at least in the way I see it, not as the symbol of poverty and human misery it has become. I'm interested in people, but also in the odd, in those who don't fit in neatly. I'm interested because their lives tell us about the society they inhabit. The tribals in Bangladesh are one example, but there are others: Muslim saints, river gypsies and transvestite prostitutes and entertainers.

By talking to and staying with different minority groups I hoped to be able to express the myths which hold the place together, and the ideas which pull it apart.

It was to be my final involvement with Bangladesh, a chance to see and do all the things I'd never had the time or the opportunity to do before. By the time the journey was over, and written up, I expected to have nothing left to say about the country or its people.

1

A Way Back

In matters of survival and personal comfort Peter's quicker than I am, so I didn't immediately realize why he'd nabbed the aisle seat on the plane. Only as I arranged my yellow duty-free bag did I notice that the man next to me was wearing a white Muslim skull cap, and bore an uncanny resemblance to some of the crueller caricatures of the Ayatollah Khomeini. Peter smiled at me, as though to say, 'Have a good trip', and involved himself in a thick book. I grimaced back; the thought of passing the next eleven hours squashed in beside a fanatical Muslim was not a pleasant one. It was little comfort to reflect that the man was probably equally displeased at finding himself next to a decadent Englishman whose merrily clinking bag proclaimed him an unashamed alcoholic – at least in his eyes.

I even caught myself wondering about bombs.

I discovered that my neighbour was a Bengali, and that he was travelling with four other men. They were all similarly attired: white skull caps, white pyjama trousers and shirts, and thick grey waistcoats which buttoned up to the neck. They also all had beards, showing that they were *haji,* that they'd made the pilgrimage to Mecca.

When the air hostess distributed lunch my neighbour stood to confer with his companions – for some reason the group had been scattered over a number of rows. They agreed not to risk the possibility of ritual pollution by eating meat prepared in an insufficiently Islamic manner, even though we were travelling on an Arab airline, which they might have expected to be sensitive to the requirements of Muslims. The men collected their plastic trays carefully, handed them back to the hostess, and asked her to provide them with vegetarian food.

This did not go down well – perhaps the hostess was insulted, as a Muslim herself, by their suspicions. She told them that if they were vegetarians they should have said so when they checked in, then suitable arrangements could have been made. She spoke to them in Arabic; fast, guttural and dismissive, and then repeated it in English. The repetition seemed to imply that they couldn't understand Arabic properly, and that there was therefore some doubt about their claims to be true Muslims. She flounced away, but after some time did produce some dry, unappetizing sandwiches.

This wasn't the end of their difficulties. As the sun set they nodded at each other then stood and started to unroll prayer-mats in the aisle. The air hostess stormed down from the galley, and insisted that they go to the rear of the plane.

The commotion woke Peter, who looked around a little wildly as he fumbled for his cameras and tried to calculate light settings, angles and the risk of detection. I told him that if he attempted to photograph the men at prayer we would swap seats, and he could endure whatever consequences there were until we reached Calcutta. He thought about it for a moment, grumbled and went back to sleep.

A few rows in front of us was a family of Londonis, Bangladeshis who've settled in the UK. There was a frail old grandmother, in an all-enveloping black *burkha,* a grossly overweight mother, also covered from head to toe in black, three small daughters, and a teenage son. The girls were dressed in loose clothes made from some material which bore a close resemblance to silver foil. It needed constant adjustment to prevent it from creasing. Even the smallest girl was well aware of the importance of a smart appearance, and kept pulling her loose trousers into a more pleasing or straighter line. It was the son who was in charge; he bossed his mother and sisters about, and intervened in all their dealings with the aircrew and other passengers, explaining that neither his mother nor grandmother spoke any English.

The family was fair skinned and good looking; high cheekbones, neat, regular features and almond-shaped eyes. The contrast between this family and the *haji* on my right couldn't have been greater. He couldn't have been described as good looking by even the kindest critic. His skin was dark and pockmarked, and his large, curved nose hung over loose lips and a stringy white beard.

Finally boredom overcame the fearsome image all Muslims have acquired since the Rushdie affair, and I asked the *haji* some polite question. Speaking softly and gesturing at his companions he answered in clear, unaccented English, telling me that they were on their way to Calcutta to deliver speeches or sermons and to discuss their faith.

'We are all followers of the Prophet. The young man behind us was an aeronautical engineer with British Aerospace for ten years before he gave it up to follow Allah. He had a brilliant career ahead of him but he saw the light.'

'And I? I am originally from Dhaka in Bangladesh. I was a diplomat until Bangladesh split from Pakistan in 1971, then I joined the British civil service. I took early retirement a few years ago so that I could travel and talk to friends, to people, about Allah.' Again he gestured at the other skull-capped figures, 'We have all given up our former lives, our homes and whatever wealth we may have acquired, in order to learn, to study and to pass on the fruit of that study. Sometimes, like now, we are invited to speak.'

Wondering whether he belonged to an Islamic political party, one of the many allied to and bank-rolled by Iran or Saudi Arabia, I asked what he thought of one such fundamentalist party in Bangladesh, the Jamaat Islami.

His response was immediate and contemptuous. 'God is not a means to power or to wealth. The Koran is not to be used by opportunists for political ends; it is the word of God. Such political parties have nothing to do with religion, but much to do with money.'

His name was Hassan, and he was beginning to interest me for he didn't conform to any of the popular images of Muslims.

My next question was another attempt to place him, or his ideas, and he greeted it with a smile. His answer convinced me that he was a Sufi, an Islamic mystic and humanist – the Zen masters of Islam who sometimes provoke and shock.

In return he questioned me about my reasons for visiting Bangladesh, and I lied easily, saying that it was a holiday, that I was visiting friends.

Hassan had launched into a sermon. 'The truly religious person has nothing to do with power or money. They are anathema to him. Possessions consume the possessor. Maybe a man cannot sleep, so he goes out and spends £500 on a new bed. He gets it home, up the stairs and into the bedroom, but when he lies on it he still can't sleep. He has to take a sleeping pill. So what use is his new bed? Why did he waste £500? He could have taken a sleeping pill and slept on the floor.'

In the seat beyond Hassan sat another Bangladeshi in jeans and sweat-shirt, who caught my eye, smiled and glanced upwards, as though to say, 'Just our luck to have to sit next to this fanatical fellow.'

'The purpose of life,' continued Hassan, 'is not to build up a bank account, to save up money or to become the owner of a house and a car. The purpose of life is to work for humanity through the worship of Allah.'

He had turned towards me in his seat, intent on the message he was trying to get across, but interrupted himself to say, 'I'm boring you, you want to read your book, or to watch the film perhaps?'

I reassured him, encouraging him to continue.

'Every living creature has a purpose. The fish in the sea, and the plants and animals on land are here to serve mankind. That much is clear. So then we must ask what we, the highest creation on earth, God's greatest creation, are here for?'

He paused long enough for me to answer, but I had so many dis-agreements with this hierarchical view of the world that it seemed better to keep quiet, guessing that a truthful reply would distress or distract him.

He answered his own question. 'We are here to serve Allah, or God. That is our purpose on earth, that is why we are here. Just as everything in the world is below us so we are below Allah. Even a savage in the jungle who has never had a chance to read the Koran or who has never heard the name of Allah, is worshipping Him if he merely looks up in admiration and wonder at the stars.'

The next time Hassan got up to confer with his companions the Bangladeshi in the next seat swopped, assuming that I would prefer to listen to him, someone from the same secular world as himself, rather than the bearded *haji*. Or perhaps he just wanted some companionship. He was thirty-two, and came from Newcastle, where he had his own clothing business. He talked easily and told me about his impending divorce, admitting happily that it was his fault ('I'm a bit of a bastard I suppose,' he said), and about his expensive car and big house. He wasn't boasting, just defining himself as an ordinary Brit., as he would have said, insisting on the difference between himself and such old-fashioned types as Hassan.

He owned, or was in the process of building, a house in Dhaka. He was going to live there for eight months while his divorce went through, and planned to study law when he returned to Britain. In Dhaka he intended to pass the time writing erotica. He had nothing better to do, he said, adding that his model, his favourite writer, was Anaïs Nin. He told me one of the stories he was going to write down: it involved the sexual humiliation of his wife and crashing his father's car. To him it was an amusing tale to while away a few minutes with a stranger, and he told it loudly, laughing heartily, as he might have laughed telling it to his mates in the pub.

It was an odd re-introduction to Bangladesh. Neither the Newcastle manufacturer nor Hassan was recognizably typical, and only the Londoni family came close to what I thought of as Bangladeshis.

12

From Calcutta we caught an early train to Bhangaon, on the Indian side of the border; from there a rickshaw carried us along a road lined with Brazilian rain trees, and blocked for a mile or more with trucks trying to get into Bangladesh.

We passed through customs without a check and were pointed in the direction of the Bangladesh immigration office where a military officer was ensconced behind a wide, glass-topped desk. Our conversation with him meandered aimlessly; he asked no leading questions, and wasn't interested in us. I'd forgotten how easy Bangladesh could be, how officials were still impressed by foreigners, how any policeman or army officer could become polite and hospitable, keen to please, when faced by a foreigner, a white. A few weeks later, when we were detained by the army in a prohibited area, this same delicacy of feeling prevented the officers from searching us properly, or at all. To some extent it made our trip possible.

My interest was not only in Bangladesh itself, but also in the collision between the cultures of south Asia and of southeast Asia which takes place along the country's northern and eastern borders. The subject is one fraught with controversy and difficulties. Neither the Indian, Burmese nor Bangladesh governments wants it discussed.

The border region is sensitive. In all three countries there are tribal insurgents and liberation struggles, and the situation is confused by the plethora of different ethnic groups – Rakhine, Chakma, Mru, Tippra, Mandi, Mundai, Khasi – to name but a few, all with their own languages and histories.

In a petrol station we found a bus going to Khulna. It was temporarily occupied by four young women, and we joined them on the shady side of the bus, listening to their raucous laughter and tough talk. The smell of the coconut oil they used to make their long hair shine permeated the air, that and the stink of diesel. They teased the driver, and told each other jokes.

'He speaks Bengali like they do on the BBC,' one of them commented when she heard me exchange a few words with a boy selling green coconuts. She didn't mean it as a compliment; it was the equivalent of saying 'He's a toff'.

The women talked, occasionally tossing a word or two, like a sweet, in our direction. They weren't like the Bangladeshi women I remembered; they weren't afraid of anything, and they shouted like fishwives at a student who tried to take one of their seats.

The student talked loudly, in English, impressing his audience, until one of the women told him that I could speak Bengali. He instantly declared that I was his friend, his master and his life-long confidant, and compelled me to take his address. 'When you return to London you will send me one watch, costing not less than fifty dollars . . .'

My surliness finally drove him away, or perhaps he had work to do for he insisted on our ever-lasting love for one another.

2

Numerous Nameless Places

As soon as I stepped out of the hotel in Khulna I was surrounded by rickshaws, circling me like birds of prey. Forgetting the most elementary rule – establish a price before setting out – I climbed into the nearest one and asked the driver to take me to Port Road.

After ten minutes I was getting suspicious. Khulna is a small place, the hotel was near the river and Port Road sounded as though it should be close by.

'How far from here?' I asked.

'Why? Don't you know where it is?'

'Yes, of course I know,' I lied, fearing that he'd start a tour of the town if I admitted my ignorance. 'Don't you?'

'Yes, I know, it's not far.'

Another ten minutes passed and it became obvious that neither of us had any idea where we were going.

We looked at each other accusingly, then asked directions from another rickshaw driver, who demanded to know who I wanted.

'Hayatt Hossein.'

'The *nayeb*?'

'Yes.'

'What do you want him for?'

'What's that to you?'

He laughed, and after adjusting his plastic, fur-lined cossack hat to a more rakish angle – the temperature was in the eighties – he pointed back down the road. 'Hayatt Hossein lives there. The house with the stairs. Just go up.'

A flight of crumbling stone steps led up the outside of a large white-washed building and onto a veranda, beyond which was Mr Hossein's office. He'd organized our steamer tickets from Khulna to Dhaka, and although I'd never met him I thought I knew what to expect. I was wrong.

Hayatt Hossein looked as though he'd stepped out of the eighteenth century. His long black hair was brushed neatly back, so neatly that it had the appearance of a wig, and I suspected that it was dyed. His mouth was wide and sensual, and he was dressed in an Achkan jacket, buttoned to the neck with gold. Across his waist hung the thick gold chain of a fob watch, and he had on patent leather pump shoes. It wasn't surprising that the rickshaw driver knew him, anyone who dressed as he did would be well known. He'd been the *nayeb,* landlord's clerk, to the Khulna raja, and as such had once been a powerful man in the district, for he'd effectively controlled the financial affairs of the raja's estate.

He stood when I entered the office, 'Come in Mr Rolt, I've been expecting you. Sit down please. You are most welcome. I am coming with you in one moment, please wait a minute.' He gestured generously at a choice of chairs.

The room was tall and had once been painted with ochre distemper, now patched with damp near the ceiling. Three glass-fronted cupboards filled with ledgers surrounded Hossein's desk which was covered in papers, and yet more papers were piled on the floor. Almost buried behind a mountain of books sat an assistant, listening meekly to his employer, who suddenly switched his attention back to me.

'When the British were here we could all learn English,' he said without preamble. 'Then we had many good English teachers. It is important to learn English. But with Independence in 1947 all the teachers went to India, all the teachers, then all the engineers, and all the clerks ...'

'They were all Hindu?'

'All were Hindu, that's why they went to India. Then again in 1971, with Liberation from Pakistan we lost the engineers all over again. All were Pakistani. So twice now we have won independence, and both times we have lost.'

Mr Hossein had much to say and enjoyed saying it. 'Then again we could all know Shakespeare, Wordsworth, Keats.'

He adopted a pose.

'In solitude

What happiness? Who can enjoy alone,

Or all enjoying, what contentment find?

Ah! *Paradise Lost,* the greatest poem in the English language. Don't you agree?'

But he was off again before I had time to reply.

'Now we cannot even get English books, all were looted from our houses during the war with Pakistan. I myself had the *Complete Works of*

16

Shakespeare, but it was looted and sold in the market. The pages were torn out and turned into paper bags. I bought some biscuits wrapped in Shakespeare's immortal words only the other day. See how cultured we are? Even our biscuits are blessed by Shakespeare.'

He grinned at the fancifulness of this idea, displaying the wide gap where two front teeth should have been.

I asked whether he had children and he jumped on the question.

'I do, and they can hardly write a letter in English. I have four children, all are at college and hardly can they write in English. What is worse is that they do not want to. They don't mind. Our college boys and girls are just cheating, and the teachers are just ignorant.'

He wasn't angry or ranting, but I tried to divert him by asking some polite question about his wife.

He leapt up, his energy was boundless. 'Yes, yes, come this way please. She is here. Here. Have a look.'

I rose reluctantly, expecting to be introduced to some shy, reclusive woman who didn't want to meet a foreigner, but followed him into a second room where his wife sat cross-legged in the middle of a double bed. He insisted that I should sit next to the bed and it was only then, when I was close, that I realized her mind had gone; her eyes were vague and unfocused, and although she smiled it wasn't at me, or at anything in particular.

'She has been like this for ten years now. Brain haemorrhage. She cannot dress, or do anything for herself. You see she had high blood pressure and our women are quite backward. Backward, I should say, because we have made them backward. So how can they learn? We have kept our women like pigeons in cages; as a result they cannot be free and they cannot learn. It is our fault. She is a Hindu, I married her in 1947, against the wishes of both families.' He jumped up, 'Come on, come and have some tea.'

We hardly had time to drink our tea before he had picked up a cane – it had a silver handle and ferule – and was marching through the office. I had no idea where we were going but it was clear that I was to follow. He hailed a rickshaw from half-way down the stairs outside, and had negotiated a fare, pulled up the hood and climbed in before I had a chance to ask where he was taking me.

We passed the administrative centre of the town and he fulminated against the local administration. 'The chairman of the municipal corporation is an illiterate muscle-man. Yes, a muscle-man who takes money from everyone. That's all he is.'

17

'Here is the *maidan,* and you see these big stands and signs? That is because the Prime Minister was here. He comes once a week now. Previously he would come once a year or less, but now these politicians are travelling the country by helicopter at the drop of a hat. That is all they are doing.'

'Stop here!' he commanded suddenly, and the rickshaw driver pulled up in front of an elegant, colonial-style building with a brick path and a well-tended garden.

I insisted on paying the fare and Hossein told me to give two *taka* (50 *taka* = £1). I did so and the driver complained to him; Hossein pointed at me and said, 'Tell him, not me. He's paying.'

'Beggars,' Hossein continued, 'that is what this government is making us into. We are all learning to be beggars because the government wants it. The more beggars there are the more money the government gets from your country, the USA, Sweden and all the others, so many countries. The ministers and officials steal three quarters of those millions of dollars, and barely one quarter reaches the poor people it is meant for.'

He walked briskly down the brick path, swinging his cane, past a notice which informed me that this was the office of the Bangladesh Inland Waterways Transport Corporation. As he'd already given me the steamer tickets I wasn't sure why we were there, but there was no chance to ask him; he was still talking.

'When I was a young man, sixty years ago, we were not even allowed to set foot inside this building. I mean us Bengalis. Your British forebears would kick us out even if we put a toe through the gate.'

He said this without malice; it was just his way of giving me the history, filling in the details.

In the office of the steamer company sat the usual fat man behind a desk. On the walls were photographs of the company's ships, including the magnificent *Kiwi,* a paddle-steamer built on the Clyde, which still makes the run between Khulna and Dhaka.

We were introduced, and the conversation drifted round to writers and poets. Hossein gave us an exhaustive list of English poets, starting with Shakespeare. The fat man sighed and looked out of the window, until he interrupted Hossein's list to tell me that his favourite British writers were Tolstoy and Hemingway. Hossein seemed embarrassed by his friend's ignorance, and there was a silence so I asked where the steamer stopped.

'Chalna, Mongla, Barisal and Chandpur.'

'Nowhere else?'

'Oh yes, numerous nameless places.'

It was the reply of urban, educated Bengal, to whom the rural areas and rural people are uncountable, anonymous and inexplicable.

As the conversation floundered on I realized that we had nothing to do there; it was a courtesy visit, to introduce me to the man who'd sorted out the complicated process of acquiring steamer tickets from Khulna to Dhaka. We had little to say to one another and Hossein soon decided that it was time to leave. He led the way through the town on foot, straight-backed and formal, an impressive figure. No one in the crowded bazaar gave his bizarre outfit a second glance, although they all stared at me as we wove our way through the areca nut wholesalers' market. Bundles of the orange and green pods, the size of plums, spilt over the footpath like green-tinged brass coins, while the traders lounged indolently, gossiping and spitting streams of red *pan* juice into the gutter.

Without a pause to see if I was still following, Hossein plunged down a narrow gully (once again I had no idea where he was taking me, or why). Stevedores packed the alley, rolling oil drums and carrying great hessian sacks of grain on their heads. The fact that they were trying to come the other way didn't affect Hossein, who marched straight on as though the lane was empty; miraculously the sweating, sun-blacked, muscle-bound men stumbled out of his way, and I followed in his wake. He also had the confidence of an eighteenth-century gentleman, someone who didn't think about the possibility of the lower orders challenging him. He assumed the privilege which comes with wealth and education; his attitude was a kind of innocence, and therefore a protection.

We emerged onto an iron floating dock, an antheap of activity; more stevedores, with loads on their heads or on trolleys, and ferry passengers who made their way gingerly through the chaos, lugging bags and bedding rolls. Small boys wreaked havoc by playing tag through the crowd – half the fun was in avoiding the blows occasionally aimed in their direction. The scene was medieval, an impression heightened by the presence of the great teak cargo vessels, the *talash,* on the river beyond, riding proudly at anchor. Around them the grey water teemed with ferries, dinghies (the word is Bengali) and other trading boats loaded with bricks, bales of jute, sacks of grain or trees cut from the mangrove swamps of the Sundarbans nearby. The *talash* were black from stem to stern, coated in pitch, and their powerful lines swept forward and up to a sharply pointed prow. At the stern their low cabins were delicately carved and decorated or painted in primary colours.

Moored against the floating dock was a small white-painted steamer, the *Moinamati*; our transport to Dhaka. It had four first-class cabins, a big hold and larger second-class accommodation. The third-class passengers could opt for the hold or the flat iron roof.

The *Moinamati* wasn't due to leave until 6.00 a.m., but Peter and I shifted our luggage on board, so as to avoid having to get up early in the morning, and settled down with a bottle of whisky to watch the sun set over the river, where freshwater dolphins played among the mooring cables.

We substituted green coconut juice for water and this went so well with whisky, that we were still there at 2.00 a.m. A few yards away one of the deck hands lay on a mat muttering to himself.

'Allah says drink is bad.

Allah says you'll die if you drink whisky.

Allah is great.

Allah!'

Mixed in with this were bits of prayer in Arabic, exclamations and deep sighs. Just as I thought he'd gone to sleep he started to chant.

The Bengal boatmen's songs, made up on the spur of the moment, are famous; they're usually about the pain of separation or the harshness of a boatman's life, and I once heard one which was a complaint against a neighbour who'd refused to lend the singer some salt.

The deck-hand also had a specific complaint:

'Oh foreigners why can't you understand me?

Because you're English and I'm Bengali.

But why don't you stop talking

And go to sleep now?

Then I could go to sleep also.

Oh foreigners I'm very tired,

I must go to sleep,

And anyway you shouldn't drink whisky,

It's very bad for you.'

On the floating dock beside us was a generator, and three men stood next to it having a shouted argument; over that racket came the thunderous reverberations of oil drums being rolled down a steel ramp, and the crash-bang of bales of cardboard being loaded into the hold.

The first-class passenger leaning against the *Moinamati*'s railing pointed across the river dotted with foreign ships, unloading their cargoes into wooden lighters. 'You see that village over there?'

The village he was pointing at was more concentrated than most; the thatched huts were packed closely together, as though for protection.

'It's where the prostitutes are. Mongla is a big port now, and sailors are always wanting prostitutes. It's an example of a village which has developed itself – in no time it has sprung up without any help from outside. Five years ago there was no village here, but without anyone making a plan, or getting foreign loans the village has built itself. It is private enterprise.'

The *Moinamati* slewed round in the river. As we came up to the quay, sideways on, my eye was caught by a woman dressed in a scarlet sari, and masses of gold-coloured jewellery. She was with two other women, and when one of them caught sight of me she waved vigorously, nudged her friends and swung her hips in a camp sort of way, I waved back a little nervously.

An official checked everyone's tickets as they stepped onto the gangplank, and then when the three women minced up to him he refused to allow them on board, pulling, pushing, and generally manhandling them in a light-hearted way. He even shouted at them as though genuinely scandalized that they didn't have tickets. They were easily equal to his game and slapped and pushed him back. Eventually they retreated giggling, but waited for their chance and rushed up the gangplank under cover of a line of porters carrying sacks of grain. The ticket collector managed to get in a couple of good slaps as they passed, but he wasn't really trying to stop them.

As we pounded out of Mongla and into the mainstream of the river I went up onto the roof deck, to look more closely at the three exotic creatures.

From there the horizon was made up of coloured strips: grey water, terracotta bank, green paddy and a black, thunderous sky into which the *Moinamati*'s painted funnel coughed thick, oily smoke. The three women sat demurely on the deck behind the bridge, out of the wind. They attracted a little attention but none of it was hostile, although I've seen women abused for less. These three had been behaving outrageously by the norms of Bangladesh society – I loved it.

They were self-sufficient and uninterested in what was happening around them. It was the wrong time to try to talk to them, but as I left the deck I noticed another woman sitting quietly on a mat by herself, brushing her long hair – the public display itself a provocation to some Muslims – and painting her nails.

I returned to our cabin to try and put Peter in the firing line, to persuade him that we should have photographs of our fellow-passengers. After a short discussion in which he insisted that he would need my help, and rejected the suggestion that I'd only get in the way, I agreed to try and manage the crowds.

Our strategy was to take photos of everyone else and then the prostitutes, as to photograph them alone might have provoked the Muslim prayer contingent, who'd just finished praying on the roof. The steward acted as a marshal and generally made everyone look as unnatural as possible, but the crowd got overexcited and out of control. Everyone wanted to be in each picture, and the boat was in danger of tipping over as they pursued Peter from one side of the deck to the other. When I asked the women whether they'd mind a photo they posed prettily in front of the funnel, while I tried to keep everyone else at bay. I was so preoccupied that it didn't strike me until we were escaping the picture-crazy mob by running back to our cabin that the prostitutes had unusually deep voices.

'They're *hijra*!' I burst out. Peter looked blank. 'Transvestites, eunuchs, hermaphrodites, men dressed as women, who knows? Maybe they work as prostitutes as well, but *hijra* dance and sing at weddings and when a child's born. They're very secretive, and don't like people to know much about them.'

I was excited. I'd always wanted to meet and talk to *hijra,* but before I'd only glimpsed them slipping through the market, and once posing at a wedding. On the *Moinamati* they were captive to my inquisitiveness.

My ship-rail acquaintance came up and told us that *hijra* frighten people. 'If you're rude to them, they can be four times ruder back. They always travel in groups and if they want something they take it. First of all they ask nicely, but if it's not given quickly they'll take ten times what they need, smash the shop, and even create chaos by exposing themselves.'

'And they work as prostitutes?'

'How can they? They're not women,' he replied in all seriousness. 'But they are very suffering people. Sometimes they force their way into a house where there's a new baby and play with it, throw it around until they're paid to leave. If the family won't pay they threaten to kidnap the child. Sometimes, if they're trying to get money by being rude, they're beaten; it's a fine line between getting money and getting blacks and blues.'

I prepared myself for talking to the *hijra* by going down into the hold, which was packed with people sitting and lying wherever there was space, on sacks of grain and of onions, cardboard bales and oil drums, all thrown higgledy-piggledy together and piled up to the roof. Here a group of men played cards, there a couple sat in silence, watching their child scramble over the cargo, and there three old peasants discussed the price of rice.

None of them had the same attitude as our fellow first-class passenger. They regarded the *hijra* as part of life, as people who shared the same fears and who were driven by the same motives as they were. Becoming a *hijra*, they told me, was just another way of surviving, and they recognized, or at least understood, the desperation which could force people to such extremes.

Most passengers were asleep, huddled up against the cold, by the time I returned to the exposed roof deck. We were approaching a small town, and the lights hung in a line before us – as though we existed on one plane only, in two dimensions between black water and black sky. The steamer's searchlight was suddenly switched on, destroying the illusion, and it played along the riverbank, then shot out across the river to illuminate a small sailing boat in our path.

The *hijra* who'd been brushing her hair earlier in the day was hunkered down in a corner, still by herself, and I squatted down nearby to see if the other passengers would react. They didn't so I edged a little closer, but stayed a respectful distance.

'Where are you going?' I asked.

'Dhaka. And you?'

'Dhaka too.'

'Where are you from?'

I asked all the obvious things, discovered her name was Leila, and then ran out of courage. I was about to abandon the idea, having realized the impossibility of asking anything interesting, when a man came up and started to point and laugh at us.

Leila abused him roundly. Her delivery was loud, vehement and fast. 'You're only laughing because you'd like to be sitting where this foreigner is,' she told him. 'Yes, you laugh but you want me ...' There was more, but I couldn't catch it and anyway the man had had enough. He slunk off into the safety of the shadows, shamed by the obvious truth of what she'd said, or shocked by her vulgarity.

One of the crew approached and sat on the mat next to her. She indicated that I should join them. 'This man is very bad,' she said. 'He's not married but he has two women, one in Mongla and one in Dhaka. Don't you think that's bad?'

'She's lying, it's all lies,' he responded, and turned on her. 'Anyway, look at you, talking about me in that way when this foreigner has his hand on your leg.'

It wasn't true, and Leila was incensed. She hit him hard on the chest, picked up her bag and dumped it between us. 'There! See? He can't even touch me, and anyway why are you rubbing your knee against me?'

Again her line of invective lost me, and again it was effective enough to drive the man away.

How do you ask a *hijra* about being a *hijra*? Especially if she's not camping it up, I wondered.

'Why are so many people rude to you?'

'Why do you think? Because I'm a woman ...' She shot back, then asked whether I'd take her to England.

'I can't. What would you do there? It's cold. You wouldn't like it.'

She was looking at me hard, and her eyes seemed full of tears – not because of my refusal, but because they were like that. She couldn't have been more than sixteen. 'Are you married? Do you have a girl in England?' she asked.

So I said I did.

There was silence apart from the sound of the engine driving us up river, and the swish of water down the sides of the ship. I was at a loss, and decided that I'd have to get to know her better.

'Where do you live in Dhaka?'

'Badamtoli Ghat. The right side of Badamtoli Ghat.'

She was watching for my reaction; Badamtoli is the red light district of Dhaka.

'That's all? I ask for Leila?'

'I live next to a shop selling attar of roses. When will you come?'

'In two or three days' time. If it's not a problem for you.'

'Not for me. Come at six o'clock in the evening, that's the best time. You will come won't you?'

Only then did it strike me; she wasn't a *hijra*. I'd been so carried away by the other three – who were *hijra* – that I'd assumed she was one too. In fact she was an ordinary girl, a prostitute, and she'd started to need me to be nice to her. I'd treated her as a human being, and she was so desperate, so hurt, that she'd trust anyone who was polite to her for five minutes.

It was raining as we moved up the Buriganga towards Dhaka, passing acres of brickworks, their chimneys belching smoke.

The *Moinamati* rounded a long, slow bend and Dhaka's waterfront slid into view. For most of the city's history the Buriganga, which loops its southern edge, has been the road by which invaders, pirates and rebels have attacked. For all its size it isn't a real river, merely a linking stream between the Brahmaputra and the Meghna. Even so it's quarter of a mile wide at Dhaka.

The river, as usual, was so crowded as to be almost impassable and the *Moinamati* sounded its fog horn continuously. Every kind of boat was there, from the rusting hulks moored in the centre of the river to Arab-like dhows, sails billowing, and the piratical motor passenger boats, which forged up and down regardless of everything else.

As we heaved into view like a hippo, dozens of rowing boats set out from the shore, wide-bellied craft lying low on the water. They approached like attackers, coming at us from all directions. The captain maintained a steady course towards this mass of predators, and it seemed impossible that none would be swamped by our bow wave, or disappear beneath the keel, to be pulped like the rafts of mauve water-hyacinth through which we'd ploughed unheedingly on our way north.

Dhaka's waterfront came closer; it's not a particularly prepossessing sight, although the noise, the colour and the confusion would delight a child. The buildings are old, but most are falling down, blackened and crumbling.

When we came level with the Dhaka nawab's palace I didn't recognize it for a moment. The last time I'd seen it the building had had the grandeur of all big ruins: trees grew from its rotten brickwork, squatters inhabited its reception rooms, and like an ancient wreck it stuck out of a sea of shanty houses, built from bits of plastic, corrugated tin and cardboard. The palace's once stately steps leading down to the river had collapsed, and it seemed only a matter of months before the building itself would sink into the mud beside the river.

The vision before us bore no resemblance to that wreck.

The squatters had been cleared out and grass planted where the shanty-town had stood, the brickwork had been repaired and, most remarkable of all, the whole, massive construction had been painted virulent pink. Restored to its original vulgarity it looked good in the sunlight which had forced a way through the clouds.

The dinghies came alongside and their owners clung onto the *Moin-amati*'s lower deck while passengers elbowed one another aside for a clear leap. The moment they were safely in the boats they settled down, and arranged their bundles, bags, chickens, and in one instance, two goats. Some opened black umbrellas. These escapees were the passengers without tickets, who had to get away before we finally docked. There were more of them than fare-paying passengers.

Above the noise of the engine came other sounds, the first in days: air horns of trucks edging their way down the dockside, the incessant, cheeky, answering jangle of rickshaw bells, the thwack of women beating clothes at the water's edge, and the delighted screams of small, naked boys diving from the massive anchor chain of a hulk moored in mid-stream.

On the dockside all was confusion. This is the city's business centre – not business in the sense of offices and banks, but of the transport, the buying and the selling of goods. From storehouses ranged along the dock road bananas, pineapples and sacks of rice spilt prodigally into the light. You could almost hear the money changing hands, of great wads of dirty *taka* stapled together in thousands. No one doing business down here trusts banks; it's cash or nothing.

When we docked, with a terrific clang and scrape as the *Moinamati* rammed the floating iron pontoon, passengers streamed off and porters leapt the rails to reach First Class before their competitors.

After two days on board, with nothing to look at but the river, the sky and boats it was difficult to step into the maelstrom of Old Dhaka, to give up the calm.

We fought for a three-wheeled baby-taxi and whizzed through the city. The overwhelming impression was of men doing business, haggling over prices, arguing and shouting. Even in a dark street selling perfumes – the shopkeepers looked sickly or drugged – the customers were all men. The few women around were either trussed up in black, or so poor as to be barely clothed.

There was only one person I wanted to see in Dhaka: Mukta. We hadn't met for two years, and much had happened since she'd left Europe and since I'd moved back to London. Once I'd seen her there would be no reason to stay in Dhaka, and Peter and I could continue our journey, to meet and talk to all sorts of Bangladeshis; *hijra,* river gypsies, tribals, peasants, politicians and Muslim saints.

3

Chittagong

Sitting on Dhaka Station drinking a quick cup of tea before the train left for the southern city of Chittagong I watched a couple take leave of each other. The woman was in tears, and as the man tried to comfort her in an ineffectual way – the station was too public a place for him to touch his wife – a smartly uniformed soldier marched up the platform, arms swinging. He halted in front of the couple, crashed his heels together, brought his right hand up in a salute, laughed, shook hands with the man and delivered a message. A second later the train hooted, and the army officer followed me on board.

'Hello, my name is Captain Akbar,' he said, holding out his hand. 'You are going to Cox Bazaar?'

It was a statement really, everyone goes to the longest uninterrupted beach in the world, and I admitted that we were.

'In Cox Bazaar there is no problem. You must stay in the Hotel Simon. It is where everyone stays. I will get in touch with you there.'

I made a mental note to avoid it, but his next few words clarified the position.

'And even if you are not there I will find you. I will know where you are.'

Producing a wallet stuffed with photographs of himself as a cadet, himself with friends, himself and his wife, of his marriage, he emphasized the significant detail with a thick, be-ringed finger, 'These are the presents,' he said, pointing out a car, a wooden bed, a table, a steel cupboard, and a stack of video equipment. A family portrait put me on my guard because in the background was a lake, hills and jungle. The only place it could have been was Rangamati in the Chittagong Hill Tracts. Suspecting a trap, I admired his wife's sari, the jeep they were standing next to and the colour of the bougainvillaea pouring over the building behind them, studiously ignoring the setting – as though it meant nothing to me.

He let me finish, but he was leaning forward keenly and he stabbed at the interesting hills and the lake. 'It is Rangamati. I was stationed there for two years. That is the Kaptai Lake. Perhaps you are going there?'

Outside the slums and bustees, the huts made of bits of cardboard, hammered tin and plastic, which coat the rail line like a nerve sheath on its passage through the city, had given way to a sheet of water, stretching as far as the horizon.

'I don't think it's allowed is it?' I replied cautiously, because we did intend to go there – knowing it to be strictly forbidden.

'If permission is granted.'

'Ah, yes, well, I don't think we'll have time.'

'Your friend is a cameraman?'

'No, no. He just likes taking photographs of his travels to show the children at school when he gets back. There are many Bangladeshi children in the school where we work.'

'You are teachers?'

'Yes,' I lied.

To my surprise this satisfied him and he relaxed. 'My wife,' he said expansively, as though passing on classified information, 'is an MA pass in English from Dhaka University.' I tried to appear amazed at his good fortune. 'You saw her at the station. She was weeping because I am leaving her for one month, then she will join me in Cox Bazaar. I have been seconded to the Bangladesh Border Defence Forces for six months.'

I wasn't sure whether this was a good or a bad thing, it sounded a little like demotion, but I nodded encouragingly.

'Her father, my wife's father, did not want us to marry, but then I told him that I would die if I could not marry her, so he agreed.'

'Really? Why didn't he want you to marry his daughter?' This may not have been a discreet question, but it was safer than talking about the Chittagong Hill Tracts, where a war has been going on for the past fifteen years between the tribal inhabitants and the army.

He slipped the photographs back into their wallet and placed it next to his heart. 'Because at that time I was not a Captain.' He frowned – his feelings swept across his face, he had no idea of hiding them. 'Bangladesh has many problems. The main problem is that everyone is corruption and we are a very poor country, but everybody is corruption.' His brow knitted further, in anger, and then, perhaps worried that I might misconstrue his statement as defeatism, he added sternly, 'But our morale is high. It is sky-high. Yes, it is higher than even the stars.' And the frown turned into a sunny smile.

'You mean in the army?'

'Yes, in the armed forces. The civilians too are keen, of course.'

'Of course.'

He was very hospitable and insisted on treating me to a bottle of 7-Up, which was fetched by a sad-looking boy of about ten. 'That boy is my servant,' he explained. 'The army gives us one servant each. This boy comes from my family's village, and his father works for us also.'

He couldn't stay off the subject of the army for long. 'Do you know that my name, Akbar, is the name of a Mughal emperor?' He sat up a little straighter. 'When my son is grown up he too will be in the army.'

The scenery passed at anything between ten and thirty m.p.h.; island villages marooned in a sea of water, in which grew the magnificent red water lotus, so large and succulent it looks edible. The water-logged fields beside the railway turned into a long canal, which had been almost emptied of water. Children, stuccoed with mud, waded around up to their thighs, grabbing at the drowning fish. Those they caught were slipped into aluminium cooking pots which floated on the stew of mud and water hyacinth beside them. The canal went on and on; in places whole villages had turned out to participate in the catch, they packed the sections which had been dammed off, wielding cooking pots and triangular nets, having a party.

As the sun and the temperature rose I drowsed, nodding awake only when Akbar came back from somewhere and sat heavily beside me. He leant over and said confidentially, 'Ten days ago I bought a Kelvinator refrigerator,' then sat back to enjoy my reaction.

I was a little slow but eventually realized that I was to respond with congratulations.

'They offered me a Kelvinator or a Mitsubishi, but I said no, I wanted a reliable one. A Kelvinator is reliable, no?'

This time I was quicker to assume a positive role, and assured him that it was the most reliable in the world, but disappointed him by underestimating its cost.

As we pulled into Chittagong he pointed out the cadet college where he'd trained. This got him terribly excited, although he did realize that I might not share his enthusiasm for assault courses.

'I am a Captain already, and I am only twenty-seven, and next month I will be promoted to Major,' he boasted.

I hesitated to suggest President before he was forty, and this private joke turned sour as I wondered how many tribal people he'd killed, how many tribal women he'd raped or children he'd bayoneted. If he'd been based at Rangamati for two years he was likely to have been involved in at least two major massacres of tribal people.

On Station Road in Chittagong every inch of pavement was taken up with street vendors. They sold green coconuts, lungi, cloth, oranges, bananas, padlocks, combs and knives, cigarettes, and sugar-cane. Each one had his patch, and his patter. There were also some striking beggars, and a *kabiraj,* a traditional healer, who sat on a mat on the pavement looking fierce, surrounded by unsavoury, though no doubt essential, bits and pieces: part of a pangolin, some scraps of fur (unidentifiable), and a few herbs, sticks and bottles. He wasn't doing much business. Another, a fortune teller, had a couple of green parakeets which had been trained to walk down a line of airmail envelopes and pick out one – the colours of the envelopes, spread like cards, and of the birds, attracted the eye, and he did a good trade. Inside each envelope was a card with a fortune typed on it, but you couldn't keep the card, you had to give it back once you'd read it.

The only thing the street lacked was women; they had little chance in a conservative city like Chittagong and stayed at home, unless they were well protected by a black *burkha,* or had no choice. Was it for this reason that the tension on the streets was palpable? Everyone seemed to want to know everyone else's business – there was a sense of urgency, of seeking, and I was made aware of the pressure of existence, of the sheer difficulty of surviving, and of the competition. The tension was increased by the fact that the opposition parties had called a general strike in response to the previous day's 'unprovoked police firing' on a demonstration in the city.

As we fought our way through the crowds to the Hotel Manila a series of rickshaws passed; the first carried six forty-foot bamboos, and their owner; the next three sacks of potatoes; another four skull-capped Muslim gentlemen – three sat uncomfortably on the seat built for two, and one faced backwards on the driver's seat.

The exuberance of life here made it bearable – to the outsider – that and the light; coming south on the train I'd realized again just how much water there is, how Bangladesh is really *in* the Bay of Bengal, is part of that great mass of water. The light in Chittagong, and everywhere else in the country is like that in the middle of a sea, not land.

Our room was on the fourth floor with a view of Station Road – probably the noisiest street in Chittagong. Outside the hotel men were erecting a blue and white awning which filled the pavement and half the road. The significance of this escaped us until it was too late.

A fellow guest in a loud, red-striped lungi and white vest was also watching the speeding traffic and the sunset beyond. He rubbed his eyes, yawned and said, 'In England all the roads are as wide as our Station Road, even your village roads are four lanes. No?'

'No.'

'No?' He looked at me doubtfully, as though I might be an impostor, but decided to give me the benefit of the doubt. 'Unfortunately we cannot afford to widen them here, although Dhaka is a different matter because of course we must show the world that Dhaka is a capital city like other capital cities, and so the norms are not applying. We must have big, wide streets to show the world, whatever the cost.' But the inconstancy of the mob depressed him. 'The common people are always letting us down, even they do not care.'

Below us a man loaded two tea chests precariously onto a rickshaw, then jumped on the rear axle and poked his head through a hole in the hood. The driver stood on the peddles to get the machine moving, and they disappeared down the road.

The man in the lungi scratched his head and made a half-hearted attempt to change the subject by asking what I thought of Bangladesh. But the common people weighed on his mind and he carried on before I'd uttered more than half a sentence. 'There are more bad people here than anywhere else in the world. Naturally, because only a fifth of the population is educated and the rest are bad.'

'I don't think education makes any difference . . .'

'Yes, yes, of course it does. You are not understanding.' He sauntered off into his room, pushing his great belly in front of him, and returned a moment later with a copy of the local paper. 'There, see what it is saying here.' He thrust the editorial at me, and I read enough to see that it was an argument for the genetic inferiority of the majority of the population. It ended with the warning that these inferior beings would one day take over – perhaps it was this which had sparked his anger. 'You see? It is they who always are giving a bad impression to the world. Even in my home town I once saw a rickshaw-wallah ask an English lady for ten *taka* for a ride which should have cost two *taka* only.' He became quite vehement, his hatred and fear of the poor evident. 'So I took the rickshaw-wallah by his shirt, like this, and I said, "Why do you do this thing? You give us a bad name to the world", and I commanded the lady to get in and to pay two *taka* only, maximum three *taka*.'

In response I told him stories about London taxi drivers doing the same thing to foreigners arriving at Heathrow, adding that for them it wasn't a life or death matter.

'But that is fair because it's all on the meter, and the profit is not excessive. The driver must still pay for petrol and so on.'

Sweat counted for nothing with this man, who turned out to be a District Food Officer; pity those poor dependent on his benevolence for their daily ration of wheat or rice. He was puzzled about one thing though. 'Mrs Thatcher,' he said, 'is a wonderful woman, but she is making a hat trick of her adamancy not to have sanctions in South Africa. Why is this?'

I told him that the workings of the woman's mind were beyond me, and once again he looked at me as though I might be masquerading as 'an English'.

The sunset had reached a crescendo of orange and red, covering half the sky. In the street below the traffic ground, hooted and screeched its way down Station Road. The blue and white awning had been fully erected, and from one end came the ominous sound of someone blowing into a loud speaker and counting, 'One, one, one, two, three, four ...' The amplification was so great that the distorted roar almost drowned out the traffic.

I pointed down at the awning. 'What's happening?'

'It is Jamaat Islami.' In other words the fundamentalist Islamic party which Hassan, my neighbour on the plane, had described as having nothing to do with God or religion, and much to do with power and money.

The Food Officer continued, 'They are having a meeting tonight. They will be saying prayers, making speeches, recruiting and such things.'

Peter had already set up his camera and was photographing the warm-up to Jamaat Islami's idea of an evening's entertainment; on the pavement four floors below our room two buffaloes had had their jugular veins slit, and their hot, scarlet blood streamed into the gutter.

Unable to stand the sight or the smell I went out, and in a tea shop near the hotel I got into conversation with two young men. They discovered that I'd taught at Chittagong University twelve years ago, and one of them peered at me more closely and then grabbed my hand. 'Mr Francis? Yes, I thought ... I was one of your students. Ahmed, perhaps you remember? But you had a moustache in those days. By the way we very much appreciated your novel, *The Last Armenian*.'

I was astounded that he should have heard of it. 'You read it? Where did you get it?'

'Yes, we all read it. It is available from the British Council, but only under the counter as it is about the Chittagong Hill Tracts and the tribal people. That is a very sensitive subject ... You know perhaps. Our country ...' He smiled deprecatingly and shrugged as the sentence ran out. What was there to say? It had all been said before, and still the politicians were shouting, stealing and doing nothing.

The other joined in. He was tall and well built, and from his face I guessed him to be Burmese, or a Chakma from the Hill Tracts.

'Yes, it's difficult to be an outsider in this country. I know because I'm a Buddhist, a Rakhine. Our people fled from Arakan in Burma two hundred years ago and settled to the south of here. My family live near Cox Bazaar.'

He didn't feel secure in Bangladesh, he told me, and wanted to leave. His people faced a lot of prejudice. 'That's why I studied Bengali so hard, to be accepted. Our language is different, it's Arakanese. Now I speak Bengali better than many Bengalis themselves. The problem is where to go and what to do. From Bangladesh there aren't many options.'

He didn't talk self-pityingly; his preference, like that of many Bangladeshis, was to laugh in the face of difficulty and disaster. How can you take such a situation seriously? they seem to ask, knowing that if you do you're lost.

'Everyone who works in government service or in an office is corrupt, and the poor stay poor. Even a peon in an office makes more money than I do; he can make fifteen hundred *taka* a month through bribery. If you're an unimportant person you have to pay the peon to get an appointment with the person you need to see. Even the university lecturers are corrupt because parents pay bribes to get their children admitted. Bangladesh is a terrible place.'

We tucked into our *gulab jamoon,* one of the fat, juicy, sugary milk-sweets which Bangladeshis adore, washing the stickiness down with gulps of thick, hot tea.

He checked that no one else in the place was paying us any attention, and lowered his voice. 'In the towns the problem is not so great, but in the rural areas we face real problems. Only yesterday, in a village called Unipara a few miles from here, some Muslim villagers attacked the Buddhist temple. They killed the monk, and injured more than forty Buddhists.'

'Was it reported?'

'Only in one newspaper, not on the television or radio of course. This kind of thing is happening more and more frequently. In other places this month there have been anti-Hindu riots, and the worst have taken place around the village homes of government ministers.'

I asked whether I could meet his family when I went south, but he said that it was impossible.

'My family is too poor. What would we do with you?'

I couldn't convince him that they wouldn't have to do anything, that I'd lived in poor villages before.

'We'd like to introduce you to someone, a friend of ours,' my ex-student said, and when I agreed they took me to a house in the heart of Chittagong, in Feringhee Bazaar.

The friend was a Chakma, a tribal from the Hill Tracts. He was a bag of nerves, and told me that he had so many false names that he couldn't remember them all. 'The army now makes it impossible for any young, educated tribal man to stay in the Hill Tracts, many of us are living in Dhaka, or have fled across the border to Calcutta. But they have nothing to do there. No jobs, no money, no life. You can imagine how bad things must be if we feel we must leave to survive.'

He tried hard to avoid emotive language, and I didn't like to ask personal questions for fear of opening old wounds. All I had to do was listen; that in itself was a cathartic action. 'There are so few people, almost no one, who I can talk to about our situation. Most Bengalis don't want to hear about murder, rape and dispossession, and anyway who can I trust?'

He talked about the Vietnam-style cluster villages put up by the army in the north, into which tribal villagers are herded – for their own protection of course – after their land has been forcibly taken from them and given to Bengali settlers. 'So we have become one hundred per cent dependent on the army. Those in cluster villages have no land and no means of earning a living. The army feeds them and decides what they should do, where they go, who they can meet. And this system is described as development. The government shows these villages off as proof of what it's doing for us! This is the democratic Bangladesh supported by foreign aid.'

He laughed bitterly, and continued, 'Every educated, male tribal is seen as a potential leader, a possible guerrilla, and we are harassed, beaten, held without trial and sometimes tortured or killed. Our women are raped, forcibly married to soldiers and converted to Islam or killed. On the one hand the government destroys tribal society and culture, and on the other claims that its treatment is generous. And most of the foreign embassies, consulates and aid missions seem to want to believe it.'

He was angry and scared. He couldn't see any way out for himself or for his people, but he had faith, too much faith in my power to influence events.

The buffaloes had been cooked by the time I returned to the Hotel Manila, and parcels of meat and rice were being handed out to the poor who crowded the hotel entrance. The attitude of the Jamaat Islami officials who organized the distribution was that of Victorian social workers, or some of the more dubious charities. They lashed out at the crowd with wooden clubs, beating women and children indiscriminately, and laughed at a teenage girl in rags who wept at the blow she received.

They treated the poor as only the most desperate would allow themselves to be treated.

In the officials' eyes the mob didn't deserve anything; the food was being donated not as an act of social responsibility, but for the greater glory of Allah, and out of the purity of the organization's corporate soul.

At three o'clock in the morning Jamaat Islami's amplified hectoring from the tent below our room was still going on, prompting Peter to remark, with great restraint and a determined lack of comprehension that, 'This kind of thing belongs in the mosque; they're committing a public nuisance.'

Jamaat Islami believes that Islam goes far beyond the mosque, that without Islam there's no life, no existence. Many, perhaps most Bangladeshis would agree that the party is a public nuisance, but few would dare say so.

We were woken a bare three hours later, at six o'clock in the morning, by someone banging on the bedroom door. When Peter opened it a boy waved a broom at him, indicating that he'd come to sweep our room. He was pushed out again with a minimum of delay and the door was closed in his face.

'Horrid youth,' muttered Peter getting back into bed.

In Chittagong I wanted to try and arrange a trip to Cox Bazaar by salt boat. Ever since I'd first seen the salt boats in the harbour I'd wanted to sail on one; they're the biggest and most impressive of Bangladesh's sailing boats, and there are fewer and fewer of them as engines take over.

What few contacts I still had in the city weren't encouraging.

'Do you want to die?' asked one. 'Not only that, it will be most uncomfortable, and if you don't sink then the sailors will throw you overboard for your cameras and money.'

I knew that he was the wrong person to ask about such a trip, but it was difficult to know how seriously to take such warnings. I was certain that, like everything else in Bangladesh, there was a key.

We started by finding our way down muddy, dark alleys, past wooden warehouses fringing the river, to Majhighat, to the salt docks. There we talked to the owner of a salt-washing factory, to labourers and to loafers, but it proved impossible to find the salt traders themselves.

Conditions at Majhighat were positively medieval. A heavy grey mud, which contained the salt, was shovelled out of the boats' holds into a pile. From there it was weighed into the labourers' head-baskets, each one containing thirty-seven kilos. The men, sweating under the weight and with salt-saturated water running into their eyes, took a wooden spill from a clerk sitting under an umbrella, then holding the basket steady with one hand, and grasping the spill with the other, they ran up the alley and into the factory. Once they'd got rid of the mud they gave the spill to another clerk, who put a mark against their name in a ledger. The operation was quick and efficient, a system which had been in operation for centuries, perhaps since the early fourteenth century, or before, when the first Arab traders reported Chittagong as a great port – even Ptolemy marked a city in the same spot.

The salt traders themselves were always away, or asleep, or just not available, and I was beginning to despair of ever making the trip, when we were invited to lunch by some friends. I found myself sitting next to a small, good-looking man with bushy eyebrows, who had a tendency to ask questions like, 'What is love?', or 'Why are women a mystery to men, when men are not a mystery to women?'. He loved music and was, he said, a romantic, a Bohemian, adding, 'But not fully Bohemian'.

He was startlingly forthright in some ways, freely admitting that the fact that his ex-wife had come from a wealthy family of Chittagong traders had played some part in his decision to marry her but, 'She knows only money. I cannot hate her although I hate the way she used me. She never had love in her life, so how can she know what it is? She was ugly, and her parents are ignorant people, rich but without education.'

His wife's parents had sent her to school in England when she was in her early teens. At eighteen she'd wanted to move to the States, but her father had insisted that she should come home and get married first, to a Bangladeshi, preferably someone from Chittagong. Faruq had turned up at the opportune moment, saying that he would be happy to live in the States, and they were married.

Afterwards Faruq realized that he didn't want to leave familiar Chittagong, his friends, or his mother. The couple had a child, and then he'd made an enormous financial loss in his business. His wife, perhaps

believing that it was a terminal loss, chose that moment to leave for the
USA.

Faruq shifted wildly between wanting her back, and talking in romantic
terms about other women.

He could talk women all day. 'Our women,' he said, 'have raised the
modesty which is demanded of them to a high art. Within the limits of
that modesty they can be as alluring and seductive as any Western woman
in a short skirt and T-shirt. Unfortunately it's difficult to get to know
women in our society because free-mixing isn't allowed.'

'Talking of which, do you know any *hijra*?' I asked brightly.

Our host nearly choked on his fish, and our hostess's already enormous
eyes grew even bigger, 'Francis!' she said, laughing, 'What are you saying?
Well, OK, Faruq is a Bohemian, and we are perhaps not quite like most
other people in this town, but *hijra*! Of course we don't know any, no
one knows any!'

Asking whether anyone knows any *hijra* is like asking a family man
whether he knows any prostitutes. They aren't the kind of people respect-
able citizens are supposed to know. However, Faruq was able to tell me
that they hung around near the Hotel Manila, dressed normally, as men,
but with heavily made-up eyes. 'If you want to meet one go down to Nala
Para, near the Lion Cinema, but don't go at night. It's a dangerous place.'

'What about salt traders? Do you know any salt traders? We want to
go from here to Cox Bazaar by salt boat.'

'Why?' Faruq asked.

'No reason. For fun. I've always wanted to do it.'

'It may be possible. I know one or two of them. I'll introduce you, and
you may discuss it. I'll come to your hotel tomorrow at three o'clock.'

After we'd taken leave of my friends I fell into conversation with a boy
carrying an empty basket on his head who was walking in the same
direction, towards the ethnological museum. He told me that he came
from another district, and that he recycled paper and tins (with lids only)
for a living.

'Why couldn't you do the same job in your home district?'

'Because there's no money there. My family live in a village, and the
nearest town is not as big or as rich as Chittagong.'

Deciding that it was too hot to walk I hailed a rickshaw, agreed a fare
of six *taka* and got in, inviting the boy to join me.

He had nowhere to sleep other than the pavement, but was reasonably
content; he'd eaten enough every day since he'd arrived in the city, which
hadn't been the case at home. 'Here, with luck, I can even save a little

money, and perhaps one day I'll be able to do something else.'

His life on the streets, uncertain though it was, seemed better to him than that led by his parents in the village: a life of continuous, grinding poverty from which there was no possibility of escape, and no hope for improvement.

When we arrived at the museum the boy jumped down and produced six *taka* before I did. He would have paid the rickshaw driver too, if I hadn't stopped him. Six *taka* was about half what he expected to make in a day. He wasn't the complaining kind; he didn't ask me for money, didn't pity himself, and perhaps even thought himself lucky.

I followed a group of barefoot urchins, carrying luridly painted catapults, into the museum, where they paid the fifty *paesa* demanded, and reluctantly give up their weapons to the safe-keeping of the guard. In the entrance hall was a large printed notice in Bengali and English about Bangladesh's tribal peoples, who it described as having, 'Little advanced from the Neolithic primitive social pattern of life'. Worse followed: it went on to describe the original, tribal inhabitants of northern India and Bangladesh, the Santals, as an 'immigrant tribe', and their unique and complex culture as, 'a somewhat half-baked civilization of the plain'.

Whether this was premeditated distortion or wilful ignorance is hard to say, although I'm inclined to believe the former. The government wants the tribal people and all minorities to be perceived as ignorant savages, with no culture or society of their own; as people who willingly embrace the dubious benefits of Bengali, Muslim culture when they're offered the opportunity by a kind and caring government. This view was confirmed in Sylhet later, in the Manipuri village we stayed in, where our host told us that he'd invited the director of the museum to visit his village, to see what it was really like, but the director hadn't been interested.

The place had been updated since I was last there; there were more photographs, and more tribal jewellery and finely embroidered cloth. But ugly mock-ups of 'Chakma village life' still dominated, and the street boys gaped, pointed and giggled at the leaden casts of semi-naked women in short skirts. I wondered whether the improvement in the museum's jewellery collection had anything to do with the destruction of tribal society, and how much of the material on display had been looted by the army in the past few years.

At the desk, on the way out, was a 'Foreign Visitors' Comments Book'. Inside someone had written, 'A shame that the government is murdering the people of the Hill Tracts as well as paying for this nonsense', and a German had scribbled, 'The tribes must survive!'. Small gestures.

4

Salt Boat

The boy couldn't have been more than fifteen, but his eyes were outlined with kohl and he winked archly as I passed, then followed me round the corner and overtook, waggling his bum. He stopped a few yards in front, turned and asked softly, 'Are you looking for something?'

I had gone out in search of *hijra* but I didn't want to say, 'Yes, I'm looking for you.' It might have started us off on the wrong foot, so I shook my head and continued on into Nala Para, where Faruq had told me the *hijra* lived.

It was night. The street was lit by the odd fluorescent tube, and by hurricane lamps that hung in shop doorways, and that swung beneath the rickshaws which skimmed by, ferrying passengers to and from the docks. Faruq had said not to go there after sunset, but I couldn't imagine going in search of people of the night during the day. It would have seemed all wrong. I stopped at a stall selling hot, spicy split peas on leaf plates and bought some, but there was no one to ask. At the counter of a cake shop opposite the Lion Cinema Hall a young man with a pointed nose was eating a piece of cake and drinking a Coke. The cakes on sale were unappetizing shades of pink and green, but I ordered one and poked at it with the spoon provided.

Conversation with the man proved sticky. Yes, he said, he lived locally. Yes, his family did come from that part of town. Yes, he was a businessman, he imported bicycle parts from India and China. No, business wasn't going well, no one had any money and his competitors were cutting their prices.

I suggested that businessmen were like farmers, that things were always bad. He smiled for the first time, but disagreed.

There was no way of bringing the subject slowly round to *hijra*, so I asked him straight out whether he knew where they lived and whether he'd take me there. He didn't seem to be surprised or even interested until we'd walked down a couple of narrow alleys, then he stopped beneath a flickering street lamp and interrogated me. Who are you? Where did you learn Bengali? If you once taught at the University who do you know there? Why do you want to meet *hijra*? What are you doing in Bangladesh? What are you going to do with the information? Finally he was satisfied and he pointed down a lane a few yards away.

'They live there, but you can't go.'

'Why not?'

'Because the place has a bad reputation, drinking, drugs and murder. The police have said that no one can go there unless they live there. But it's OK because one of them is coming now.'

A slight man in a lungi was walking slowly towards us. His hair was tied back in a ponytail, and he stopped when the cycle importer spoke to him. We were introduced there on the street.

I was unprepared. This wasn't where or how I'd expected to meet a *hijra,* and I forgot simple Bengali words; our conversation was stilted and difficult. After a few minutes a warm drizzle began to fall, and the cycle importer left us in the middle of the dark alley. It wasn't long before a group of children, street kids who knew Nargis, the *hijra,* rushed up to us.

They were high spirited and happy, demanding to know who I was, where I was from and so on, and they joked about the crowd of us standing in the rain. They were friendly children, but they all talked and shouted at once, making conversation with Nargis impossible. He said, as though he'd reached a decision, 'Let's go and drink some tea. We can talk more easily without them.' Until then he'd been distant, uninterested, but perhaps because I hadn't been rude to the kids, people like him, from the same class – with nothing – he'd been convinced that I was OK.

'No, no,' the children chanted, hanging on to our clothes. 'No, come back, you can't go!' But they soon found something else to absorb their energies.

He led me to a partitioned-off booth in a tea shop nearby, of the kind used by families, or couples, to shield the women from the stares of strangers while they eat. He didn't draw the curtain, and allowed me to order tea and a *paratha* for him. At a table outside our booth sat two fat businessmen dressed in cream silk pyjama suits, stuffing food into their mouths as though they hadn't eaten for a week. They ignored us entirely, deeply involved in a discussion of money.

Under the lights Nargis seemed sadder than he had in the street, and his clothes, a blue shirt and a lungi, were more obviously worn. Around his neck was wrapped one of the patterned cotton scarves popular among the poor all over north India, Nepal, Pakistan and Bangladesh. They must be uncomfortable in the hot, humid weather but they're often the first non-functional status-symbol to be acquired by men with sixty or so *taka* to spend on an extravagance. The first two status-symbols are at least hypothetically functional: an umbrella and a watch (working or not).

Nargis wanted to know if I spoke Hindi, and was disappointed that I didn't.

His long hair was oiled flat and once or twice he ran a hand over it, to check that it wasn't out of place, as he talked to me across the table. It was an involuntary, feminine gesture, one which had become natural. His black-shaded eyes were deep and seemed somehow to retreat at the slightest sudden movement or noise, although his body stayed rigidly erect. It was as though he'd trained himself not to flinch, to keep his mind free of what was happening around him. He may have been floating free on opium, but I couldn't be sure.

He was forty-five, or thereabouts, and his father had worked as a deck hand on the steamer which plied between Calcutta and Rangoon until about 1950. The family was poor. At eleven Nargis earned a few *taka* here and there by singing, and when someone, a relation, suggested that he should become a *hijra* it had seemed like a relatively good, even exciting option.

There was no doubt in his voice when I asked whether he'd have become one if his family hadn't been poor.

'No. Never. It's not a good life, even though I've travelled all over north India, seen all the big cities and hundreds of villages.' He was silent, then spoke again, explaining or spelling it out for me. 'If the police see us together they'll arrest me. Or if I come to your hotel they'll handcuff and beat me. There are only five of us in Chittagong now. There used to be many, but it's not a good life anymore and the rest have gone to Dhaka or Calcutta. Will you take me to England when you go back?'

It was said without hope, and he was neither surprised nor disappointed by the reply; perhaps he would have kicked himself if he hadn't asked, on the off chance. He waved away my explanation of why it wasn't possible with a graceful gesture, as though it wasn't that important anyway, and broke the *paratha* so that he could dip it into his tea.

His grave eyes bored into me, and I found that I couldn't continue to question him. I felt as though I was watching an abstract of hurt, as though I was a voyeur of pain. It had been the same on the *Moinamati*, talking to the girl prostitute – and it happened once again in Bangladesh, in a tribal village on the edge of extinction.

He finished his tea, smoked a cigarette, and asked the waiter to fetch him some *pan* from the stall outside. When it came he checked the contents then put it carefully into the side of his mouth; *pan* was a luxury to take time over.

The mild narcotic effect of *pan* released something in him, and he started to talk, but in Hindi. I could catch only one word in five, and told him that it was no good, but his mind was somewhere else. He was following the trail of his life through dances and songs in the back streets of the subcontinent's great historical cities, Delhi, Hyderabad, Varanasi, Patna, Calcutta and Dhaka, and through villages not marked on maps, places so remote it would take days to reach them, and then only by boat.

He recalled none of it with laughter or a smile; not the people, the places, the clothes or the colours.

Walking back through the market I spotted a pile of persimmons on a stall and asked the price. It was too high so I continued, looking for a better deal elsewhere. No one else had any so I returned to the first stallholder. He wrapped the odd, spherical fruits, which looked like old potatoes, into a paper bag made from an exam paper. I gave him a ten *taka* note, and held my hand out for the change, but found that I'd misunderstood the price – they were even more expensive than I'd thought – I walked off, with every intention of leaving them.

On Station Road a torchlit procession was blocking the traffic. The men chanted '*Hartal! Hartal!*' (Strike! Strike!), and waved their flaring, petrol-soaked brands.

All I could think about was persimmons; strikes, processions and torches all faded into insignificance; I turned into the market once again. The paper bag of fruit was still there on the stall, and as the man took my money he said, 'It's a Bangladeshi game this. You can't beat us at it.'

The moment I woke I was aware that something was wrong, but couldn't put my finger on it immediately. The room was filled with light, and there were no unusual noises ... no noises whatsoever. The glorious, deafening silence had woken me; the strike called by the opposition parties, a total, twenty-four hour strike. What bliss not to be jerked into consciousness by the ear-splitting blast of air horns, and the rumble of trucks as the dust began to rise for another long, hot day in central Chittagong.

On the other side of Station Road the Madraj Restaurant was furtively open, its grille gates pulled to, leaving a small gap for customers to squeeze through. The boss stood by the grille ready to slam it shut and padlock it from the inside should a mob decide to enforce the strike. On a wood-burning clay stove by the entrance the cook was frying *paratha* with practised speed. His assistant piled them one on top of the other until there was a stack about ten high, then he clapped them between his hands, to make them puffy, before passing them into the restaurant. That was the assistant's sole job – to puff the *paratha*.

One or two banana sellers had set up on the pavement, and many people were walking around, some may have been going to work, but most looked as though they'd decided to take the day off. There was no traffic moving, not even a rickshaw. A gang of children was taking advantage of the empty street to play a kind of rule-less, unorganized boule with green coconut shells, and a crowd was forming around two men erecting a stage and loud-speakers down the road near New Market.

It was like that all day. Very little happened. A rickshaw driver, reckless or desperate enough to risk the roving bands of political thugs, was pulled off his machine and slapped around a bit – the tyres of his rickshaw were let down. A couple of lorry loads of police in riot gear sped past going nowhere in particular, and came back again ten minutes later, and at New Market a small, uninterested crowd was harangued by some local political leader. There was no serious trouble, and less tension than on a normal working day, although by the evening stories of riots, and of 'police firings' in Dhaka and other towns had started to circulate.

It was a twenty-four hour strike, but by sunset people were bored and hungry, and the fruit and veg market gradually opened up. As the road filled with shoppers two men set up a stall directly below our room. Both had thin, ascetic faces and were dressed in flowing white Muslim cover-alls. They set down on the pavement a small tin trunk and a large commercial cooking-oil tin. From the trunk were produced a plastic mat for them to sit on, a ghetto-blaster and microphone, and a car battery. While one fiddled with the electrics, the other placed a hardboard rectangle on top of the trunk, and then covered it with a grubby, moth-holed red cloth. Everything was done neatly, with practised precision, not a movement or a gesture was wasted; it had been done many times before, and this was what made it fascinating. It was like watching the creation of a stage-set. Rapidly then, glass jars containing tin charm-holders (suitably inscribed with the name of Allah the Merciful) were positioned at the front of the impromptu table, and a couple of handfuls were spread on the cloth, artfully at random. The men had the quick, deft fingers of card-sharps, never still; the fingers following the arm movements through, curling or uncurling, turning palm out flat, revealing or concealing. I wasn't sure which.

The mike was checked, in English, 'One, one, one, one, two, five ...' A pile of rice paper with holy verses printed in blue and red, in circular and other patterns, was placed towards the back of the table next to two stoppered glass bottles and six Erinmore tobacco tins.

The show had already begun. I was enthralled by the production; it had been rehearsed to perfection, and I couldn't tear myself away. Others had been caught too; a small crowd had gathered to watch. More treasures came out of the cooking-oil tin: a magnifying glass, and a miniature Koran. One of the men, sitting cross-legged behind the table, began to chant into the microphone, holding it close to his lips with one hand while with the other he opened the Erinmore tins, shifting them around with the dexterity of someone in Oxford Street doing the three-card trick. In each tin was a different, unidentifiable substance.

He chanted in Bengali, unrelentingly, throwing in a few Arabic and English words every now and again for greater obfuscation. It was half-way between singing and talking, with the same rhythm and pace as a Koranic prayer. The charms were sold for fifteen *taka* each, and the gist of his patter was that it wasn't much to pay in comparison with the value of a life. For their money the punters got some tiny bits of whatever was in the tins, shaved or scraped off into a sheet of prayer-covered rice paper, which was sprinkled with scented, holy water from the stoppered bottles. The paper was then neatly folded, rammed into a charm holder and sealed in with a scrape of soap.

Those who doubted were invited to inspect the tiny, printed verses on the rice paper through the magnifying glass.

The two men did a roaring trade; I counted over three hundred *taka* changing hands in the space of an hour. The money appeared and disappeared in a ceaseless flow, all to the continuous, mesmeric chant. It was as though the men who threw down their money were hypnotized, their critical faculties held in suspension by the slick double act.

It was nine o'clock and Faruq still hadn't turned up – even for a Bangladeshi with the excuse of the *hartal* six hours counted as late.

In the street was a small boy, a beggar, whom I'd managed to avoid until then, but I was thinking about something else and forgot to keep a wary eye out for him, until it was too late. One minute I was walking along a crowded street, and the next two arms had clamped themselves around my legs. I looked down and there he was.

The boy's particular trick was blackmail.

He had a physical age of about four, but was probably in his early teens. His legs were crippled and he sat on the pavement, like a spider, shifting along on his hands with great agility, waiting for unsuspecting or unwary pedestrians. After he'd grabbed someone he'd refuse to let go until a coin had been tossed into his bowl. Strangely this technique was accepted; if any other child had tried it they'd have been threatened or cuffed, but he'd been doing it so long on this patch of pavement that he was almost an attraction. And no one wanted to be seen hitting out at what was apparently a crippled baby. I dug out a coin and gave it to him, but he wouldn't let go until I'd handed over a note.

There were other beggars who worked this busy patch of pavement too. From the hotel I'd watched the most successful of them; a man with a hunched extension to his leg, like a fat torso. It was almost like two people attached by a leg. At first I thought it was elephantiasis, but it wasn't a disease – more as though he'd been born with a deformed Siamese twin. While he was thin and wretched-looking his 'other', his attachment, was fat and sleek, taking all the goodness from the food he ingested.

The man squatted on the pavement and pushed the extra bit of his body in front of him on a low trolley. His partner, a leper with no feet, went backwards, facing the trolley, dragging a bowl in one hand and a stick in the other – the stick was to beat back children who got too close. Progress was as slow and as painful as possible; the deformed man lifted his body off the ground and propelled himself and his trolley forward about three inches before repeating the process. The sight of them was so pitiable and gross (and they made it seem even worse than it was), that people paid to look as much as anything else.

There was also a man who lay face down on the pavement, without moving, chanting or speaking. He could have been dead, except that he appeared at dawn each day and left at dusk, although how he arrived or left I couldn't say. His arms stuck out at his sides, and his legs were drawn up either side of his body, while his entire head was bound up in a cloth, as though it was too hideous to display – although this was unlikely, given the power of deformity to attract cash. There may or may not have been something wrong with him; the angle of his legs was odd, and his stillness and his silence were eerie, but it was just his particular, individual trick – what he'd learnt to do for his living.

To write about the beggars in this way makes them sound important, as though they stood out on the street, as though they were the most noticeable thing there; in fact they were insignificant in the volume of colour and noise, and in the press of people. Station Road isn't quite anarchy made real, but it looks like it.

No sooner had I escaped the crippled boy than I bumped into Faruq on his way to keep his appointment with us.

'I'm sorry,' he said, 'the strike and everything. I went to see my daughter – she stays with my mother. Do you still want to meet a salt trader?'

'Yes, of course. Now?'

'Now. Why not? Come on. The proprietor of Shamsul Ahmed Traders is my friend. We were at school together.'

The dock road was silent, and I sat in the rickshaw outside a private house while Faruq went in to fetch the proprietor of Shamsul Ahmed Traders Ltd, who turned out to be none other than Shamsul Ahmed himself, a large, forceful man who strode out of his house and led the way to his office. He swung down the dark road like a sailor, and it was obvious who was in charge – Shamsul Ahmed exuded authority without having to try.

His office consisted of a bare wooden room in Strand Road. Inside was a telephone, a desk, a bench, and a couple of chairs, little else. He sent his assistant, a man as thin and slight as Shamsul was well built, out to get 7-Up for us, and someone else, the night guard, to bring a jug of country liquor, or 'country' as they called it. Only when the necessary hospitality had been dispensed, and a couple of large glasses of country had been drunk, was the situation explained to Shamsul. I could understand very little of what was said as Shamsul spoke Chittagonian, a dialect as different from Bengali as Neapolitan is from Italian, and Faruq slipped easily into the colloquial. The discussion went on and on, and more country was drunk, until Shamsul turned to me, and in easily understood Bengali tried to persuade me that it would be better to take the bus to Cox Bazaar, and then take a regular steamer to Maheshkali Island. The reasons he gave were many and various: it wasn't the salt season, the sea was rough, there was nowhere to sleep on the island, the food wasn't good, it would be a long and uncomfortable journey, and there weren't any lifeboats. Then Shamsul and Faruq started talking in Chittagonian again. Another jug of country was fetched, and drunk, and the conversation became increasingly lively. Everyone joined in; Shamsul's assistant was listened to respectfully, and even the night guard was allowed a say.

I was beginning to get bored, so in a lull in the discussion I asked Shamsul something that had been puzzling me since I'd seen the salt factories; how do you wash salt? The answer was obvious, in a hundred per cent salt solution, but my interest enthused Shamsul, who determined to show me everything. He poured a full glass of neat country, insisted that I drink it straight down, then took us to the dock so that he could explain the process properly.

At Majhighat a boat was unloading by the light of a single Petromax. Shamsul stepped confidently onto a six-inch-wide plank over a gap between the black water and the salt ship, then scrambled over the side and into a bum boat.

'He is like a king here,' said Faruq, and I could see that it was true. Shamsul was greeted with smiles and deference by the sailors, stevedores and everyone else we ran into. He even had the natural command and presence which a king should have.

Shamsul snapped his fingers and a sailor picked up the oars. Around us rose the black hulks of the salt boats, their crooked masts and thick rigging outlined against the Milky Way. There's something magical about being rowed about an alien harbour at night, filled with boats which could come from eighteenth-century London. It made me feel like a child in an imagined world. The smells disturbed and stirred by our silent progress through the water were rich; of salt, river, tar, and fish.

We were in high spirits by the time we got back to the office, where another friend was waiting. He was introduced as a poet, 'A small poet,' confided Faruq, 'but still a poet. Among other things he's translated Sylvia Plath into Bengali.'

More country was sent for. Shamsul announced that he'd arrange our trip, that we'd go to Kutobdia Island in one of his boats, and that he'd accompany us.

'He likes you,' Faruq explained. 'And it's better if he goes with you.'

'For security reasons?'

The question was translated back to Shamsul who laughed. 'No. The opposite. The boatmen are very simple people. You'll frighten them. You are from the moon as far as they're concerned. They know nothing about you.'

'We might bring bad luck?'

'No, no, nothing like that. It's just that they won't know how to behave with you. They'll be shy.'

The poet wanted to talk poetry. His favourite English poet was T. S. Eliot. I had no sensible comment to make on this, but the necessity of saying something was pre-empted by Faruq, who remarked, apropos of nothing, that Shelley liked boats.

'Like Hemingway liked guns,' I responded.

'And he's buried beside Byron in Greece,' said the poet poetically.

Foolishly, I challenged this statement, and a sterile argument ensued.

Faruq, who wasn't interested in English poets, let alone where they're buried, interrupted us to insist that the poet was his only friend. 'Of course, I like girls too, too much, but it's difficult to find a sincere girl.'

Shamsul, as noisy and enthusiastic with drink as the rest of us, elaborated on the planned boat journey. It had been taken out of my hands, and the only thing to do was to follow.

The poet informed me that Shamsul wanted to go to Kutobdia Island because he was a follower of a Muslim saint, a *pir*, who lived on the island. He wanted to visit his guru; it would be a kind of pilgrimage for him to see the *pir,* who was called Shaha Abdul Malek Kutobi.

5

Saints and Shrines

The Kutobdia Island *pir*, Shamsul's guru, was still alive, but there was a shrine of another famous *pir* in Chittagong, that of Bayzid Bostami, who died in the city in the fifteenth century. Originally from Bostam in Persia the saint had travelled the known world, performing miracles and teaching. In Chittagong, so the story went, he sat down by a pond to think but his reverie was disturbed by a flock of djinn flying around his head. The djinn were generally annoying everyone so Bayzid converted them all into harmless turtles, and put them in the pond at his feet. And there they still live, in the pond below his shrine.

The pond was dark green, murky with algae. Pilgrims, mostly women and children, stood on the steps of the pond, making oblations to the metamorphosed djinn, which were still powerful in some way, able to confer a blessing, or good luck, or respond to wishes. When the turtles emerged, floating up out of the depths like bad dreams, and came to the steps the pilgrims splashed water over their matt backs and then touched their own foreheads. It was more like Hinduism than the supposed austerity of Islam.

The turtles, enormous, greedy and diseased-looking, snapped at pieces of banana, offered to them on the end of sticks. They used to be fed meat as well, we were told, but it had been forbidden since one had grabbed a little girl's toe, taking it for a choice cut perhaps, and refused to let go. At another shrine, where there were holy crocodiles, a woman had had her arm bitten off a few days earlier.

Leaving our shoes at the bottom of the hill we climbed up to the shrine itself, passing people selling candles, incense sticks, coloured paper, and sugar sweets. The grave, covered in gold cloth, was inside a large building like a mosque. Outside it sat three old men behind a gaudily decorated wooden coffer, into which people put their offerings. Some gave money, others returned the candles or incense they'd just bought – the dream of

49

every businessmen is to receive back as a gift (unused) that which you've just sold at an inflated price. One of the men, whom I took to be in charge as he had his hands on the coffer, said that it was a universal shrine, to which Buddhists, Hindus, Christians and Muslims were welcome. His eyes were watery and tinged a pale blue, and he joked with three young women who came to buy coloured thread from him to tie around one of the holy trees outside. 'So many wishes?' he asked. 'For such young women you seem to want many things. What can they be?'

The women giggled and half-hid their smiles behind their hands, but they wouldn't tell.

The frangipani trees, which would grant any wish, were festooned with thousands of pieces of coloured thread, to such an extent that three of them were dead, strangled by the needs and desires of pilgrims. The fourth looked as though it hadn't long to live; only one branch had any leaves.

Shrines to other, later saints had been built on the same hill, and there was a constant movement of people through and around them. The followers of one saint or another sometimes stayed there for months, or years at a time. A boy took us to the grave of Professor Hariullah Master (Baba), set in a well-tended garden near the top of the hill. As he led us in he said, 'This garden is like your country; very beautiful and quiet. Here there is always a breeze and peace and shade.'

We met one of the professor's followers, a man called Khalil Rahman, who had lived on the hill for a year. 'Master Baba', as he called the saint, had been a professor at Calcutta University. 'I follow him because he foretold everything, everything.'

No clearer idea of why the professor was so great was forthcoming, but Khalil was an impressive figure himself, with bright, sparkling eyes and lots of dramatic gestures. His curly black hair was tied back in a loose ponytail and he had a substantial beard. He was a slightly frightening, patriarchal figure, an effect enhanced by his clothing, which consisted of the ubiquitous lungi and a worn, blue serge blazer with brass buttons, which might once have belonged to a railway inspector, or some similar official. This was buttoned up tightly – he had no shirt – over a variety of beads which hung round his neck.

Khalil's talk was punctuated by frequent laughter, and his self-confident presence made me feel that *pir*-ism was the interesting side of Islam, the mystical side, more attuned to the rhythm and needs of the people of Bangladesh than is the 'fugitive and cloistered virtue' of traditional, Middle Eastern Islam. It allows a largely uneducated people their eccentricities, their paganisms and their need for an approachable religion – a saint or a holy tree. It's like the iconism of the Catholic church set against the fanatical, Jesuit purity of the Inquisition. It's the eclectic end of Islam in Bangladesh; living saints and the shrines of long-dead ones are found all over the country, centres of worship and pilgrimage, substitutes, some say, for the numerous Hindu gods and goddesses.

The delta region pits its population against a nature both rich and cruel, and this, taken together with the prevailing social anarchy, has led the peasants to deify the things they fear; the spirits of tigers, crocodiles and so on, and to create a popular pantheon of *pir*, who include pioneering settlers, Portuguese sailors, and metamorphosed Hindu deities. There are historical and legendary *pir*, fictitious *pir*, universal and local *pir*, ancient and contemporary ones. *Pir*-ism provides order, authority, assurance and faith in the politically and literal shifting sands of the delta.

Khalil offered us tea, and sent a boy scampering off to the village at the bottom of the hill to fetch it. I asked him whether Bayzid Bostami or Shah Jalal, another Persian saint who's buried in Bangladesh, was the better saint. Khalil stuck out his tongue, held his ear lobes and mooed in shame.

'A teacher,' he said, after he'd recovered from the shock of my question, 'knows which of his pupils is better than another. He can say that. But what does a cow in the field outside in the classroom know? She can say that there is a teacher, and that there are boys and girls, but can she say which one is the best or the worst? All she knows is that they are all cleverer than her.'

The crew of Shamsul's salt boat were eating their breakfast, squatting in the stern, when we turned up early in the morning to catch the first tide. The river was a flat silver, broken only by a couple of the black sailing boats which had already loosed their moorings and were away, high out of the water and hugging the far bank. The early light flowed on their bulging, tattered sails and on the paddy beyond.

Peter provided much of the amusement for the journey; the quantity and technical complexity of his gear – tripods, cameras and binoculars – kept the crew interested for some time, but they were mystified by a 'Travelamok'. Peter dug it out from somewhere deep in his hold-all, and attempted to sling it between the bow-sprit and a stanchion. They thought it might be a fishing net, and couldn't think why he wanted to put it there, but assisted him with some handy, seaman-like knots. However, they fell about laughing when he climbed in – he'd strung it so low that he was more or less lying on the deck. They were much taken with the idea though, and re-tied it for him at a more suitable height. Peter, who'd envisaged a relaxing voyage, found himself watching the crew, for the most part incapable with laughter, lying in and on, and falling out of, his hammock.

I asked one crew member how long he'd been at sea.

'Since I was eleven.'

'You must have been in some storms then?'

The rest of the crew broke in at the question – they all had stories of boats they'd been on which had foundered, or broken up in storms, and I thought uncomfortably of the 220 kilometre per hour cyclone reported in the Bay that morning, even though when last heard of it had been travelling northwest, away from us.

'Sometimes, in bad weather an engine boat will jump, like a motorbike, the propellor screaming as it loses contact with the water.'

'It must be frightening?'

'No, I'm never frightened, although two boats I've been on have sunk. One got smashed to pieces on a sandbank when her rudder broke in a storm. We were picked up from the water by another boat nearby.'

Our captain was a quiet man who held the long tiller comfortably under one arm, his eyes permanently fixed on the horizon. A couple of dolphins played beside, in front and behind the boat, before getting bored and disappearing.

The men had such good eyesight that they were able to point out the island after a few hours; I could see it only with the aid of binoculars. It took the rest of the day to reach it, and we coasted down the leeward side, passing dozens of salt boats drawn up on the mud; their flat bottoms ensured that they stayed upright and dignified.

At the village of Lemshikali our captain sailed into a creek, past more salt boats, until we couldn't go any further. A dinghy was brought for us and when we'd all climbed in we were dragged through the water then pushed across the mud flats by a team of three boys – all to save us the bother of rolling up our trousers, taking off our shoes and wading, thigh deep through the thick grey ooze. We stood in the boat, being pushed across the mud, like Victorian gentlemen in a *Punch* cartoon. Only Peter and I found it odd, or amusing.

We walked a couple of miles across the flat, uninteresting landscape, past the empty salt pans – production wouldn't start for another month or so – to the house of the local big-shot, who owned all the land between the coast and his house, greatly exceeding the legal land-holding ceiling. We were followed for a short while by a group of curious local men and boys, and two little girls – too young to be shut away, yet. They were the only females we were sanctioned to see during our two-day stay on the island.

We passed a grass and bamboo hut with a pumpkin plant growing profligately over its roof, and a woman sorting rice in the little courtyard yanked her sari up to cover her face when she saw me peering over the fence.

Toward the centre of the island the bleak, grey salt pans gave way to a more lush environment, and we turned off the track down a narrow path towards a set of buildings hidden among a grove of fruit and coconut trees.

The room where we were to stay was at the back of the largest building, covering about a quarter of the area of the house. The mud walls were nearly a yard thick, and had small windows set into them. The ceiling was made of woven, split bamboo and roughly trimmed tree-trunks supported the roof.

Although there were five of us, we were unaware of any consternation caused by our unheralded arrival, although it was probably the well-hidden women who cursed, not the men – our presence caused no extra work-load for them. Most of the family had gone to another island, to take a look at the son's fiancée, and to enjoy her family's hospitality. As honoured guests a goat was killed for us, and we ate it with rice for breakfast, lunch and dinner. Faruq described this as 'traditional hospitalization', then frowned, realizing that it wasn't quite the right expression, but unable to put his finger on the mistake.

The saint, the *pir*, Shaha Abdul Malek of Kutobdia, was filling Shamsul's thoughts, and as the sun went down we set off across country to his home. The first obstacle was a deep, muddy stream which was negotiated via a bridge made of a single bamboo to walk on, supported on inverted v-shaped uprights, also made of bamboo. Another single bamboo, at shoulder height, provided a handhold, but the thing swung and bounced uncomfortably, and came perilously close to pitching its users into the mud below. Once over this we found a group of rickety rickshaws, unlike their gaudy city cousins, whose drivers agreed to take us on to the *pir*'s house.

The path was so rough that the drivers weren't able to ride for more than a few dozen yards at a time, before having to get down and drag us across the countryside, over deep ruts and sections of track made of brick, from which about half of the bricks were missing. It was a bit like sitting on top of a home-made go-cart crashing down a steep hill.

Shaha Abdul Malek has developed such a following in Bangladesh, and beyond, that he's had to construct a complex of restaurants and dormitories for the pilgrims who've made the journey to see him. There was no electricity on Kutobdia and the light from dozens of hurricane lamps shone invitingly through the lattice-work of these split-bamboo buildings. Our arrival caused intense excitement among the hundred or so boys who attended the religious school in the complex. They crowded with us across an open cement courtyard and into the administrative centre where two men sat behind a desk. The lamp was shielded with a piece of card, so their faces and eyes were in deep shadow. One was old, with a grey beard and a gentle manner, while the other, the *pir*'s son, was fat and unshaven, the vest he was wearing was dirty and his pebble glasses glinted malignantly as he interrogated Faruq about us. A less saint-like looking character would have been hard to imagine.

More and more people crammed into the room to peer at the foreigners who'd come to see their *pir*, and some even started to pull at the bamboo lattice behind us to get a better look, until they were shouted at by pebble glasses.

When Faruq told them that I could speak Bengali the focus shifted to me, and I did my best to answer their quick-fire questions, asking in return whether the saint ever talked to all the pilgrims together, or whether he only gave private audiences.

The old man replied, 'He talks to us all sometimes, but he's eighty-two now and not as strong as he used to be, so the public sessions don't usually last more than a few hours.'

'What does he say?'

'He says many things, or nothing. Sometimes he just sits and looks. He can read peoples' minds you know.'

'Will he speak tonight?'

'Who knows? He usually speaks once or twice a week, but it's up to him. If he feels like coming then he comes, otherwise not.'

'How long have you known him?'

'I've been coming here for forty years, and in fact I now live here. We're very glad you've come all this way. You're most welcome.'

'Thank you, but we're only here by chance.'

'For whatever reason you're welcome.'

I had no idea what to expect, or whether to expect anything, but was heartened when the son sent a boy to tell his father that two foreigners had come to see him. After a few minutes the boy returned.

'How did he react?' the son asked.

The boy revelled in his role, and acted the part of both himself and the

1. FISHERMAN ON THE DAWKI RIVER

2. (*above*) Banana boats in Khulna   3. (*below*) Dhaka rickshaw

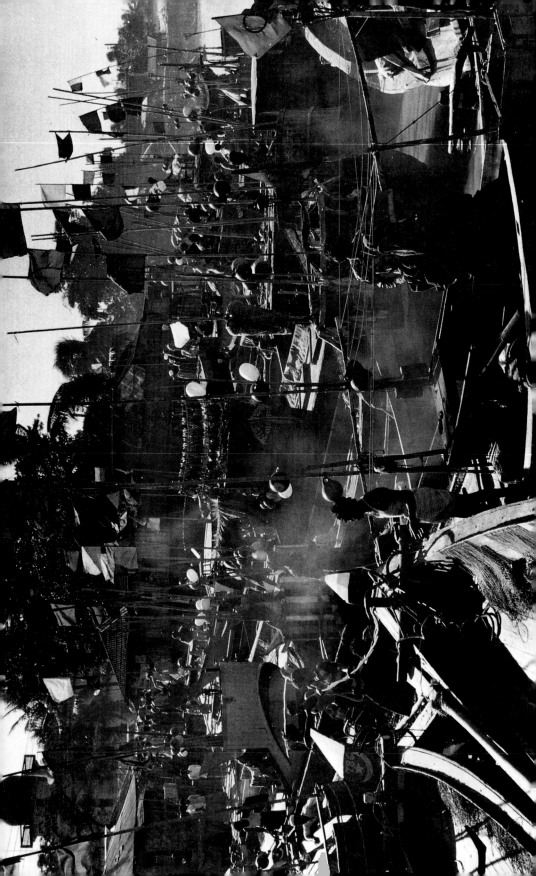

4. (*above*) Cox Bazaar harbour   5. (*below*) Fish harvest at the full moon, Teknaf

6. (*above*) Trading boats, Manipuri Bazaar   7. (*below*) Mru woman, Chittagong Hill Tracts

8. ST MARTIN'S ISLAND

saint. 'When I told him he jumped up from his bed – you know how he can be – and declared that he'd give a sermon immediately.'

Everyone except the old man laughed, and I realized that the saint wasn't an icon; he could be unpredictable and childish, even unintentionally amusing – his ways were unfathomable.

Suddenly a great shout went up. Everyone rushed outside, smiling and laughing, some were clapping, but the confusion settled down into a powerful roar, 'Allah! Allah! Allah!' Both syllables of the word were equally stressed.

The old man waited for everyone else to leave, then rose and ushered Peter and myself outside, despite our protests, 'We'll stay and watch from here. We'd be happier, really.'

But he wouldn't allow it.

There was a crowd of six or seven hundred people sitting in the courtyard. They were all clapping and chanting, 'Allah! Allah!'

The old man walked right to the front. We sat down near the back, but he returned for us, insisting that we should follow him. Somewhere behind me I heard Shamsul, unaware that we'd no choice in the matter, gasp in horror at our presumption, 'They can't go up there,' he said.

The old man didn't allow us to sit until we were directly in front of the saint himself, who sat cross-legged on a mat, theatrically lit by two Petromax lamps. He stared into one of them, entirely motionless. Beside him on the mat was a pillow, a large hookah and his shoes – a pair of rubber galoshes. He had an untrimmed goatee beard and close-shaven dark hair. I was disappointed – he had no presence in the sense that Shamsul or even Khalil, the bearded man we'd met at the Bayzid Bostami shrine in Chittagong, had presence. The saint was just a skinny old man dressed in a dhoti. He looked, to me, like an ancient and belligerent tortoise – the effect of his round head and creased skin perhaps.

The saint suddenly laughed out loud, and took a deep pull on his hookah. The smoke eddied round him and the rich scent of molasses and tobacco drifted over us. The crowd, still clapping and chanting, watched intently as he gestured and mouthed words at people only he could see. He stared harder at the lamp, smoked, talked to himself, shook his head and shifted uncomfortably on the mat, behaving like someone who's been incarcerated in an asylum too long.

The old man approached us with a brass plate, 'If you'd like to give,' he said. There were a few hundred *taka* notes and many small coins, but I had no money on me at all.

The plate was returned to the saint, who counted the offerings, and seemed to be a little depressed by the amount; he flung it away from him like a child who's suddenly got bored of a counting game.

After half an hour of chanting, the saint raised his hands and it stopped instantly, leaving my ears ringing. We were sitting immediately in front of him, but he asked a general question, as though he couldn't see us, 'I've heard there are some foreigners here tonight.'

'Yes, from England,' someone answered.

He ordered a mat, two cups of tea and some cake to be brought for us, and then signalled for the chanting to begin again. When the mat was brought it was laid out next to him, and we were told to sit on it.

We sat there drinking tea out of neat, porcelain cups while the chanting continued, wondering what the next act would be. I felt as though I'd been set up as an example of Western decadence for the faithful – drinking tea while they intoned the name of Allah the Merciful. Peter, on the other hand, was quite at ease. 'At this rate,' he said, biting off a piece of cake, 'we'll be offered a pull on his hookah.'

A beetle blundered into one of the lamps and fell to the mat, where it lay on its back buzzing and waving its legs in the air. The *pir* bent down to look at it more closely; he put his head on one side, as though asking forgiveness for being the cause of its death. His movements and gestures could have been interpreted in any number of ways, and I wondered if this was part of his success, that he was all things to all men.

Four appallingly sycophantic acolytes responded to the saint's wishes and commands – re-filling his hookah, changing the position of a Petro-max, or answering the odd question. They were odious because they were acting out a role. They ran around like children, holding their ears in mock shame and moaning when the saint snapped at them. It was like bad pantomime.

The son at least played no part in this side of things; he wandered about checking on lamps and generally ignoring the event staged by his father.

The worst of the bunch, a good-looking man of about thirty with grey hair, sat next to Peter; his deep voice, which sounded like a lorry grinding up hill, grated at every 'Allah!' Once we'd finished our tea and cake we had no excuse not to clap – in fact we were ordered to by this man. The session had lost its novelty, and was becoming tedious; the only slight, comic relief was provided by the saint, who ordered one of the acolytes to bring more lamps, until there were five lined up in front of him. He regarded each one carefully, his head first on one side then on the other, as though trying to choose one out of the five. I found myself hoping that he'd set fire to the hookah's rubber hose by bringing it too close to one of the hot lamps, which occasionally sent yard-high jets of flame shooting from the top, in the manner of Petromax.

The chanting stopped again and the saint glared, as though he'd seen us for the first time. 'Why are these foreigners here?' he asked.

'They came to see you, sir,' an acolyte reminded him.

'How did they hear about me?'

I answered this time. 'We came with a friend, Mr Shamsul Ahmed. He told us about you.'

The fact that his fame hadn't spread all the way to London seemed to disappoint him, but Shamsul and Faruq were forced to join us on the mat. Shamsul cowered behind us, genuinely frightened of the saint's power.

'What do you want from me?'

My mind was a blank; it would have been rude to say that we didn't want anything, but I managed to stammer out something about a blessing.

The saint was satisfied with this and he indicated that the chanting was to continue. It went on, uninterrupted, for the next three hours. Very little of interest or moment broke the monotonous litany, 'La, ilaha ill'Allah! La, ilaha ill'Allah! La, ilaha . . .'

But the repetition, or boredom, or maybe the saint, did engender something; I began to feel as though I'd entered into a silent dialogue with him, or a battle of wills. One minute I was thinking that he was just a mad old man, and the next, as though it had been placed in my mind, there was an idea that if I chanted the name of the Prophet along with everyone else the saint would prove to me that he wasn't mad. 'Why should I prove anything to you,' the saint seemed to be asking, 'if you don't chant for me?'

'La, ilaha ill'Allah! La, ilaha . . .'

After an hour I wasn't well disposed to the name of Allah, and after three . . .

When the saint did, finally, call a halt he launched straight into a sermon about the inevitability of death. Even he himself must die, he said ('No, no, oh no, no master,' moaned the acolytes, rolling their eyes and weeping). 'All my family are dead, everyone must die.'

He rounded on one acolyte, a fat, middle-aged man in white flowing robes and ordered him to tell everyone about a recent plane crash, to say how many people had died.

As far as I could make out it was no more profound than that, and it was soon over, to my relief.

'I shall finish early tonight,' he said, 'because these two foreigners are

57

here, and they're bored. They can't understand what's happening, so for their sake we won't go on all night.'

The saint remained on his mat while the crowd filtered out, exhausted by their efforts. Someone asked him whether he'd said the promised blessing for Peter and myself.

'I asked Allah to forgive them a long time ago,' he snapped back.

'After the last three hours I'm going to need Allah's forgiveness,' I told Peter quietly.

Faruq, on the other hand, had been impressed. He was excited and appreciative.

'But you weren't clapping or chanting very enthusiastically Faruq, I hardly saw you move all evening.'

'There's no need to hurt your hands to worship Allah,' came his dignified reply. 'I was repeating the name of Allah in my head. You know, this saint is really a holy man.'

'What about his hangers-on?'

'They are just dishonest people who want the business when he dies. For them this is an easy way to make a living. The saint plays with them, because only one person will be nominated to take over from him, and it may not be any of them.'

'He was a very brilliant student you know. Then he became mad and he was sent to an asylum where he stayed for some years. But no one could think of any reason for him to be there, so he was released again and he came back to his village home, here on Kutobdia. For years he roamed the island talking about Allah, and finally he achieved sainthood. The point is that he doesn't ask anyone to come here, or listen to him. He doesn't want or need all these pilgrims; they're a problem for him, because he has to feed two or three hundred people every day.

'The acolytes may be free-loaders, here for three free meals a day and the possibility of riches later on, but the saint is real.'

6

Monks and Money

There was little space among the hundred or so passengers, their bags and their raised umbrellas, on the deck of the steamer which was to take us from Kutobdia to Cox Bazaar. The crew insisted that no one should sit near the edge of the unprotected deck, and they herded us towards the centre.

The cyclone was still circling the bay and these boats often turn turtle, so despite the fierce sun we stayed where we'd be thrown off rather than trapped inside the boat if she sank.

We chugged south, stopping at the odd wooden jetty in the middle of nowhere, on some unidentifiable island, and sometimes at a nowhere of mud in the middle of nowhere. The boat picked up and dropped its passengers in ones and twos, like a country bus. The passengers were rarely lucky enough to be able to step directly onto dry land; usually they had to roll up their trousers, or lift their saris well above their knees and wade through the thick, black mud.

'What is Beauty?' Faruq asked at the beginning of the journey. He wanted to discuss 'girls'.

'Depends on the person who's looking, or listening.'

'I mean what girls are beautiful, and why?'

Beside us a group of five men were playing poker, snapping their cards down with much noise and enjoyment, and concealing or guarding their stakes under the mat they sat on.

'If I see a beautiful girl,' Faruq continued, 'I can communicate with my eyes alone. There's no need for talking. I can tell a girl I love her, and see whether she loves me just by looking.'

'Then what?'

'What?'

'Then what do you do? It's not significant communication is it? Once you've mooned at each other for a bit you have to do something more don't you? How long can you stare at one another? Communication is more than looking into each other's eyes isn't it?'

'It's enough to begin with. Love is the most important thing.'

'But you don't know whether your ideas match up. You might have one idea about love and she might have another, completely different idea.'

'I know Bengali girls. They are very soft and gentle and simple.'

'And I think that your ideas are so out of touch with reality that it's dangerous. Your ideas about Bengali women have been fostered by romantic love poems and songs. You can't really believe that they melt every time a man goes past.'

'No, but they lack that capacity of a man.'

'How do you mean?'

'I mean that men can love more than one woman at the same time, but women's minds cannot have that capacity.'

The boat nudged up to the land, pushing its bow onto a wide expanse of mud. On the bank a man rolled up his wide pyjama trousers and stepped confidently into the ooze. He was followed by a boy in a lungi and a T-shirt who was carrying the man's suitcase on his head and an engine-casing in one hand. The engine-casing was so heavy that it dragged the boy down into the mud; each step was an effort of balance.

'I think you'd better read some feminist books before you go to Europe. You can't say those kind of things there. You'll get into trouble.'

'Please, what is feminism? Actually I am a very simple person.'

Trying to explain the broad outline of feminism to a poetically inclined Bengali man who's never come across such ideas before isn't easy, Faruq couldn't think about women as normal human beings because he'd never had more than fleeting access to them. To him they were poetic myths; any chance contact with a woman, however slight, was loaded with significance and given a sexual charge by frustration. Not that I consider myself a particularly hard-headed realist when it comes to women. We all have our dreams.

The man had reached the boat and was given a bucket of water to wash the mud off his feet and legs. The boy was still struggling towards us; to compound his difficulties his lungi had begun to fall down. He knew that if he got the engine-casing wet he'd be in trouble, but he couldn't suffer the indignity of his lungi slipping around his ankles in full view of a boat load of people. He stopped and made a grab for it, twisted it tight around his waist and managed to get his hand back to the suitcase in time to prevent it falling off his head. The man, the owner of the suitcase, engine-casing, boy and all, had settled onto the deck and raised an umbrella – he could have carried his possessions (and the boy) without difficulty himself, but it would have been beneath his dignity to do so.

Power and status lie in what you don't have to do.

'When I am forty or forty-five I will marry again,' Faruq was saying. 'I will marry someone soft, maybe seventeen years old, someone who comes from a village. Not a complicated person, someone very simple and kind.'

He kept returning to this idea of simplicity, to the idea of the village maiden living a simple and honourable life.

Later, when we met dozens of village women and girls at a Buddhist temple we visited together, attractive women dressed up in their best clothes, Faruq wasn't impressed; they were too familiar, he wasn't charmed by their reality and presence.

'All poetry,' Faruq continued, 'and all the greatest songs are about separation, or about loss. There is a concept in Hinduism and in Bengali poetry called *biroho*, or separation, and a person who's separated from a loved one is called a *birohi*. It comes from the separation of Raddha from her loved one, the god Krishna.'

'We call it masochism . . .'

He didn't know the word, so I explained it and suggested that to spend one's time pursuing the impossible, the dream of love, was masochistic. Poetic but masochistic. He thanked me gravely for the explanation, then added, 'Anyway Raddha was made for love. She entered a holy state with her madness; it is the same madness sought by holy men, by *pir* and by the Bauls when they sing. It is madness and ecstasy joined together: divine love. I too enjoy what you call my masochistic, romantic dreams.'

'They're a product of your society and its attitude towards women; a product of religiously enforced repression and hypocrisy.'

'And your views also are a product of your society.'

This too was his charm; he never countered my rudeness with rudeness.

His questions were endless: 'What do you think of free love?' 'What are hippies/punks/mods?' (And when I gave some definition or other, 'Actually I am a hippy then.') 'Are all English girls soft and sincere like Bengali women?' 'What is a Green?'

He was an educated, intelligent man, but he had no access to information – and no real desire for it. He was interested because I was there next to him, but it wouldn't inspire him to search further. He was as uninterested in the reality of the West as most of us are in the reality of

61

the East – it's enough that it exists, and that we have certain ideas about it.

The boat was riding the waves into the Cox Bazaar estuary, and coming up the river we passed through a flotilla of fishing boats, packed up against one another, some moored to the bank, some out in the river. They were painted red and blue and green, bright, gay colours. At the stern of each boat were fixed five or six bamboo poles, striped blue or red and white, and a flag flew from every pole. They cracked and fluttered in the breeze: Bangladesh's flag – a red, Socialist sun rising over the dark green of Islam (Bangladesh was created a secular state) – the flags of individual owners, flags for colour, and flags for the fun of having flags. It was like sailing into a Kurosawa film, like a medieval armada about to set out on some vainglorious, piratical and opportunistic raid, painted in the colours of a nationalistic enterprise; for king and country, or for the greater glory of God.

There was a sense of impermanence about it all, as though the whole fleet might suddenly depart, take off in a rush without warning. Newly-washed clothes flapped in the breeze, and the fish drying on lines flashed silver, like so much weaponry – muskets or pikes. It was a temporary encampment, an army gone domestic for the day, or for however long they had – no one could be sure.

The quay too was jammed with fishing boats, and the skipper of our steamer was furious. He yelled at the fishing boats, and used his prow as a battering ram to crash into them, denting the wooden stern of one, and destroying a line of pomfret hanging along the side of another, grinding the drying fish to nothing between the two boats. It took fifteen minutes of frantic activity on the fishing boats to make room for us to tie up at the quay.

Cox Bazaar was established by a certain Captain Harry Cox in 1799 for the Arakanese, or Rakhine, refugees from the Burmese King Bowdow-phya, who had invaded and taken over the previously independent kingdom of Arakan fifteen years earlier, reputedly putting nearly a quarter of a million Rakhine to the sword in the process.

We came off the boat dehydrated and exhausted after our six-hour journey in the sun, into a street packed with buses which rent the air with their horns, and sprayed black exhaust over the pedestrians. I'd been looking forward to going to the Rakhine shops at night, to their wicker front rooms lit by hurricane lamps, but of course Cox Bazaar had changed in the ten years since I was last there. It had grown into another dusty, noisy town – it could have been anywhere in the subcontinent – and the Rakhine were hardly in evidence any more.

Shamsul decided to go straight back to Chittagong; he'd been to see his *pir*, made offerings and prayed. He'd done what he'd come to do, and he was afraid that his business would be in decline without him. We persuaded Faruq to stay with us for a day or two. He'd recovered from the depression brought on by the thought of leaving Chittagong, the familiar, and had begun to enjoy himself.

Captain Cox had ordered the jungle to be cleared, and commissioned a Buddhist temple to be built for the Rakhine on a hill above the town. The original temple had long since collapsed but there were other, more recent buildings. I walked up the fifty or so stone steps, overhung by bamboos which curled above the path like a green tidal wave, and took off my shoes as I entered the temple area. The two temples were massively constructed of wood; they were raised ten or twelve feet above the ground on posts made of whole teak trees and rose in Gothic tiers, one above the other into the blue. A monk appeared, opened one of them up for me, and disappeared into a back room without a word, but a small boy, who told me his name was Kumar, pointed out things of interest. Inside it was dark, with a row of polished brass Buddhas lined up like sentinels, and it smelt musty. In glass cases were hundreds of expensive offerings, more Buddhas, some made of silver, or decorated with precious and semi-precious stones, reliquaries, libation dishes, incensories – the objects of ritual. Everything was covered in a thick layer of dust.

I felt like a witness to the last, despairing gasps of a religion which had been stifled.

Perhaps this was what the Rakhine thought too, for beyond these two temples was a more modern shrine, where the feeling was different. The shrine was light and had a whitewashed wall around it, in contrast to the dark and gloomy temples. Enclosed within the wall was an open cloister running round a low building stuffed with images of the Buddha. There were perhaps twenty of them, made of different materials, in different positions, and the ceiling was decorated with hundreds of paper flags.

As I stood looking at the array of Buddhas, in wood, marble, lacquer and brass, a monk came up and without preamble reeled off the dates of the different images, and explained how to tell the difference between the Arakanese and Burmese styles of wood carving. He moved around the shrine with great energy, pointing out details on different images, and talking – he assumed my interest. Kumar grew bored and went outside to play football with his friends in the temple compound.

The monk wore orange, and his age-spotted skin was smooth, unshaven. A mole below his bottom lip sprouted two long hairs which curled away from his chin.

'This is the oldest image,' he said, pointing at a gold figure. 'It is Buddha touching the earth in a gesture which symbolizes his Enlightenment. This image was commissioned by Captain Cox when he built the original temple here. It is carved from a tree cut down on the site, and then covered in gold leaf.'

There was something unusual about the monk, but I couldn't put my finger on it, and I asked whether he was Rakhine.

'No, I am Burmese, from the south of Arakan. The Rakhine are very ignorant people. The men know only how to drink and are very dull. Their women are intelligent and do all the work. Arakan could be rich, but its people are slow-witted, they don't want to improve their lives.'

'It's not easy in Burma at the moment is it?'

'It's not easy, but change isn't easy anywhere. I'm in Cox Bazaar because I had to flee Burma after the government cracked down on the democracy movement. I was one of the leaders of the movement; I had forty thousand followers. Fortunately the local police chief was a friend, and he warned me that I was going to be arrested. I escaped across the border pursued by ninety soldiers.

'I was trained as a lawyer,' he continued, 'then I became a teacher and ran a school for twenty years before becoming a monk in 1975. I lived alone in the jungle for twelve years. Many times I caught malaria and cured myself with extracts from the rain tree.'

He had learnt English, he said, during the Second World War. 'When the Japanese invaded Burma I was conscripted, along with all young men, to be a porter on the Burma Road. You've heard of the Burma Road? Being a porter wasn't much fun so I ran away, and hid in the jungle. Only then did I understand that democracy is important for any society.

'Of course I know all the Burmese leaders. I was at school or university with half of them.'

He carried on talking as three young men came up and prostrated themselves in front of him, touching their heads to the ground. He seemed to find this mildly amusing, but muttered a blessing to each one.

Another monk called to him sharply, as though he wasn't supposed to be talking to foreigners. 'I have to go. I should be praying now. That was the bell a few minutes ago.'

'What's your name?'

'I'd prefer not to tell you. No one knows I'm here. Ask for the Minbiya monk if you want to see me again, but I'm going back to Burma in two months, in time for the elections.'

Kumar returned and beckoned me, 'Come and look at the stupa at the top of the hill.'

The area around the temples had been settled by Rakhine. Some houses were balanced precariously on the steep, sandy hillside leading up to the stupa while the older ones, on the level, were built in the same manner and style as the wooden temples: solid constructions of teak, supported on massive tree trunks.

Kumar led me up a tortuous path to the top of the hill, which was dominated by the whitewashed stupa. The view was of trees, and beyond them the sea. Away from the noise and exhaust fumes of the town the luxuriance of the vegetation, and the nature of the palms and flowers were more noticeable. Three or four children were flying paper kites high above us and the only sound was the singing of kite strings as they yanked down and reeled in the slack with practised speed, or sawed at their opponents' taut lines.

From Cox Bazaar the eighteenth-century Rakhine refugees had spread out through the district, erecting temples and making plantations as they went. The biggest concentration of these temples is in the area around Ramu, a few miles north of Cox Bazaar. It was at Ramu that the British had been defeated by the Burmese in 1824, in the interminable conflict between the two expansionist empires – a conflict which went back as far as 1718 when the emperor of Burma had written to the Governor General, Warren Hastings, demanding that he surrender Chittagong and Dhaka. Hastings had returned the letter with the comment that it was perhaps a forgery, and thereby sparked a war which lasted until the final British annexation of the Kingdom of Ava in 1885, a hundred and sixty years later.

Ramu is built on a bend of the main road, the only road, from Chittagong to the south. It's a small town, not obviously different from the dozens of other towns one passes through on the bus.

From Ramu Peter, Faruq and myself got a couple of rickshaws to take us to Lamapara Khyang, the largest and most impressive of the Arakanese temples. It took half an hour to reach the place, and we rode through the luminous green depths of areca nut plantations; the narrow tree trunks fell straight as plum lines from a thin canopy of leaves and plunged into the earth in a Medusa head of roots. The sunlight penetrated to the ground, striping the verticals oddly – like an optical puzzle. Set deep

65

among the shadows, in the plantations, were substantial wooden houses, the houses of a forest-dwelling people, of a people who weren't afraid of shadows.

The houses no longer belong to the Rakhine; they'd lost them at Liberation, in 1971, when some had supported the wrong side – the Pakistanis – and they were all blamed. Their lands and houses were misappropriated as 'enemy property', and their right to live in newly independent Bangladesh challenged.

A tiny and fierce old Rakhine lady wearing a black wrap-around skirt and a belt made of silver rose from the steps of her house as we came through the stone gates of the temple compound. She didn't greet us, or smile but went to fetch the keys to the two great temples beyond without a word. Her face was a map of lines, and a fat cigar was clamped between her lips.

The temples were magnificent teak structures, rising in a series of elaborately carved and filigreed stages, with steeply banked roofs. After the undifferentiated, green gloom of the plantations this clearing and its leaping architecture were intensely dramatic.

The old lady led us to the first and largest temple, rattling a bunch of keys large enough for the Pearly Gates, and with some difficulty she managed to turn the rusty lock and push open the main doors, which creaked into darkness. It smelt of damp, of white ants and of neglect, and only as my eyes became accustomed to the dark was I able to pick out the glint of gold or brass towards the back of the vast room where sat a line of Buddhas. It was like breaking into an ancient burial chamber, and finding that somehow, after centuries of nothing, of time passing, some spark remained; that there was a spirit alive still amongst the dead, abandoned things.

The sonorous tolling of a bell took us outside again, to where some small girls were playing around a stone structure supporting three Burmese-type bells, topped by a couple of fiery dragons. The children stared at us from behind the bells, but were too shy to come into the open until they realized they could talk to us in Bengali, then they were easily enticed out and held our hands as they pointed things out and chatted about school, about their parents, about anything which caught their attention.

The woman's fifty-year-old grandson was chopping wood with a machete beneath the other temple, which was built on stilts like those in Cox Bazaar. They lived there, he told us, and inside two bed rolls were spread out forlornly in a corner of the great, empty room.

'Could we stay here a few days?' I asked.

He reacted slowly to the question, but raised all kinds of objections; there was nowhere to sleep, it wasn't comfortable, there was no one to cook and not enough food. I answered each one, and the old lady finally interrupted, 'It's not possible. It would cause many problems because the government has forbidden us to allow outsiders to stay.'

Further questions on why the government had forbidden it were met with shrugs and silence, although it seemed that the woman and her grandson lived in the temple because the government wanted the site with its buildings, and the Rakhine didn't want to hand them over. No one said it, but the implication was that the Rakhine don't trust the government – they have no reason to.

The rickshaws carried us out of the magical green forest and back to Ramu, where we followed a gang of youths dancing along a path in an excited, sub-disco manner in time to some drums, cymbals and a flute. They were accompanied by a group of women dressed in their best and reddest saris, going towards a temple on the other side of the main road. They weren't Rakhine but Bengali Buddhists, Barua. The temple was surrounded by a high wall, and it was only when we came to the gate that the noise hit us.

The monks, about ten of them, sat beneath the temple in their orange robes receiving delegations of women bringing gifts of more robes, neatly folded and carried on brass trays on their heads. Others presented branches made of wire and coloured paper, and decorated with one-*taka* notes, candles, incense sticks, and exercise books. The noise was made by one of the monks who was giving a sermon, a teaching, over the loudspeaker system, which was turned to a point fractionally below feed-back. No one was paying him any attention, and in fact most people looked shell-shocked by the racket.

'If the monks had to hold their audience,' Peter shouted in my ear, 'by the sensitivity or brilliance of their discourse, rather than by sheer volume, then there might be some purpose to this. This is just a show of power.'

Faruq had a different interpretation, 'This kind of festival never used to take place on such a large scale or with so much public display, but since the Jamaat Islami and other extreme Muslim groups have begun to grow the pressure on minorities has increased. They feel the need to assert themselves more and more. They fear being swamped.'

My elbow was suddenly and painfully gripped between two strong fingers and almost before I could turn to see who it was I found myself being propelled into a quieter corner of the compound. It was a Barua monk, although two days' growth of stubble and dark glasses gave him a villainous appearance. He questioned me aggressively about what we were doing in Ramu, and when that was finished he talked about money, moving on from there to his family.

'My family has had a house in Kent near London for more than fifty years, and all my brothers live in the UK or the USA. Our village home is fitted out with all modern conveniences: full-flush toilets, bathroom and everything because my nephews are married to English and American girls and they often visit.'

He wasn't interested in the ceremony but did explain to me that religiously inclined women spin the thread, weave the cloth and dye it orange all within twenty-four hours – that's why the festival is called 'difficult orange robe day'.

Before he realized that I could understand he roughly cross-questioned Faruq in Bengali, in a way designed to humiliate, to stress the social gap between himself and our friend. It was an interrogation more than anything else, and he didn't release my arm until he was satisfied that we were unlikely to come up with large amounts of money.

Unfortunately I was destined to meet him again.

Once I'd got used to the noise, and could block it out without thinking, I enjoyed myself watching the women and the parade of cloth and gifts for the monks. I asked Faruq whether he was happy at having the chance to see so many women together.

'It's not interesting,' he replied. 'They're only village girls, very ignorant.'

'But Faruq, you told me that you want to marry a village girl when you're forty-five!'

'A Muslim village girl, not a Buddhist. I like mystery. Purdah makes women mysterious because you can only catch glimpses, or see a pair of eyes, but there's no mystery here. The girls aren't covered up; they look at me boldly, straight in the eyes, and smile. They're not shy or ashamed to look.'

'But you like Western women because they're not afraid. I thought you liked that directness.'

'Western women are different. Did I ever tell you about my honeymoon in Delhi? We stayed at a hotel on Janpath where there were Western tourists also. On the second night I came out of my room late at night to go to the bathroom and in the passageway I came across a tall, blonde Danish woman wearing only a towel. "Can you help me?" she asked, so of course I replied that I would gladly give her any assistance she required. She asked whether the manager was in his room and said she'd knocked, but that there was no answer. I didn't know, but I said that it was late and asked why she wanted the manager. She replied that the light bulb in her room wasn't working, and asked whether I could fix it for her. I was very afraid. I didn't know what she wanted. She was beautiful and I wanted to kiss her, but she was bigger than I am, and I thought that perhaps she would slap me. I told her that I couldn't go into her room because I was married, and if my wife woke up it would cause me many problems.'

'What happened?'

'I went back to my room, but I think about that woman very often. What do you think she wanted? Why was she wearing only a towel? Do you think she would have slapped me if I'd tried to kiss her?'

In Cox Bazaar the next morning the monk hailed me from a rickshaw as I wandered off to find some breakfast. He looked even more venal than before – his stubble had grown and in addition to wearing dark glasses he was smoking a cigarette in a long, black holder. He jumped down from the rickshaw and gripped me by the elbow again. I pulled away but he came after me.

'There's no future for minorities in this country,' he said. 'The government talks but does nothing. In the army, the civil service or the government there are no Buddhists, Christians or Hindus in positions of power. You probably know what's happening in the Chittagong Hill Tracts better than I do because we get no news about it here – it's all censored, or is government propaganda.

'We, the minorities, number nearly a quarter of the population, but we're ignored. The President talks about Bangladesh as a Muslim country, and he makes Islam the state religion . . .'

His grip on my elbow – it was almost a judo hold – increased painfully and he pushed me towards a nearby house, talking all the time. 'Come in here for a moment. My very good friends here will tell you. Everything I say is true. They will give us breakfast. Come.'

I was hauled unceremoniously into the front reception room of an old-fashioned bungalow. The monk settled himself comfortably, and introduced me to the woman and her husband, who waved in a friendly way while he carried on talking into the phone. They too were Barua, and unusually for Bangladesh they both worked; she was a development worker with a United Nations' agency, and he was involved in the logging business.

'That's why I formed this human rights group.' The monk was still talking to me. 'I am the treasurer, perhaps you would like to give some money? The government is afraid of us because we have a committee of famous people in the UK.'

'Oh yes, who's on the committee?'

'Well, I can't remember any of their names at the moment, but all the people of our community are facing tremendous problems. The businessmen, for instance, can't do business. They have to pay bribes to get import or export licences. To buy land for factories they have to pay bribes.'

'Surely that's normal. Everyone has to pay bribes, whether they're Buddhists, Hindus or Muslims. That's the way the country operates.'

He paused, flipped up his flip-up dark glasses and inserted another Benson and Hedges into his cigarette-holder. 'Yes, maybe, but we have to pay bigger bribes than anyone else. Ask him, go on ask him.' He gestured with the holder at the businessman, who was still talking on the phone.

I waited until he'd put the phone down and then asked him.

He was discomfited by the question. 'Actually I am facing no difficulties because I'm in business with Muslims.'

The woman came with a tray of tea and biscuits for us, and the monk insisted that they both sit down and listen to him. He spoke quickly in Bengali about his human rights' organization, at the same time writing their names in a receipt book and tearing off a slip for them. He left only the amount blank.

The woman took the slip, and fetched a five hundred *taka* note from somewhere within the recesses of the house. It was a large amount of money by Bangladeshi standards, but the monk picked it up a couple of times, and dropped it back on the table as though he'd rather not soil his fingers with it. Within a few minutes he'd talked them into doubling the amount.

I realized then why he'd taken me there, that I was necessary for his shaming tactic to work.

7

Woodcutters

Government offices close early, if they open at all, and I wanted to arrange for us to stay in a government bungalow in Teknaf, on the Burmese border, as far south as you can go in Bangladesh. I'd left it a little late to start the process of getting permission, but took a rickshaw to the Roads and Highways' Department, as I'd been told that they had a bungalow in Teknaf. The Executive Engineer wasn't there, and it turned out that they were reconstructing their bungalow anyway. The official I spoke to said that the Forestry Department had a very fine bungalow. Another rickshaw ride later I discovered that the only two people in the Forest Office who could give permission were both out of Cox Bazaar. One was in Dhaka, and the other was in Teknaf with his family.

'If you go to Teknaf today you should catch the SDFO at the bungalow, and you can ask him yourself. There will be no problem.'

'SDFO?'

'Sub-Divisional Forest Officer.'

'What if I miss him?'

'Then it's better if you go to the Water Board's bungalow. The Water Board's office is the far end of the town. Go now and you will catch the Chief Engineer.'

The rickshaw drivers were beginning to wonder what was going on. I was shooting from one end of the town to the other, to no apparent purpose. I explained what I was trying to do, and the rickshaw driver told me that the only way to get permission was to go to the District Commissioner himself. This was confirmed by some young men hanging around in the Water Board's forecourt who refused to tell me where the Chief Engineer was. 'Go to the DC,' they said. 'His office is near the court building.'

It was the other end of the town of course.

The District Commissioner's office was a concrete block – a building in which to house, or hide a bureaucracy. A uniformed guard at the entrance told me that the DC was on the fourth floor, and at the top of the stairs I asked a peon to direct me. He looked both ways down the long corridor, open on one side to the sky, as though the DC might be lurking nearby, or he might find inspiration from the brass name-plates on the doors. Outside each door was a square, red-painted flower pot containing a fern or a palm. The peon pointed confidently to the far end of the corridor, 'The last door on the right.'

It didn't look hopeful. None of the offices I passed were occupied, although all had impressive-sounding designations on their brass plates. True to form the DC's room was also empty and locked.

A kind businessman took pity on me and whisked me down a floor to meet some friendly senior official who made two telephone calls and told me to go back to the Water Board, where he'd arranged for the Deputy Director to give the requisite permission.

From there on it went like clockwork. The rickshaw returned me to the far side of town, and at the Water Board I fell in with an old clerk who wanted to talk about two hundred years of British rule before he'd release me to the Deputy Director. I said that it was all over now, history, finished and done with, but that wasn't how he thought of it – his early years had been spent in government service under the British, and he wanted to say how good it had been. Or at least pretend to me that it had been good.

The letter I eventually received was written in Bangla and English and stamped twice. It requested the Sectional Officer of the Water Board's bungalow in Teknaf to 'do the needful', and allow Peter and myself to stay.

Somehow the day had passed, and I walked to the sand dunes by the beach, carrying the valuable letter, to watch the fishermen throwing their weighted nets into a liquid sunset. They stood on a sand bar fifty yards out from the shore, ignoring the crowds of Bengali honeymooners and holiday-makers – women in black *burkha* splashing around in the shallows. The fishermen walked through the sea with the slow high-stepping gait of water-birds, their nets over one shoulder, and caught a few pathetically small, minnow-like things.

Down the beach came men carrying bundles of wood on their heads, or slung from a pole supported on the fatty tissue at the back of their necks. They shifted the pole across from one side to the other as they went, and had a fast, bouncy walk, timed to the spring in their poles. Their feet were bare, and made deep marks in the wet sand. They had half-walked, half-run ten miles from the jungle, having spent the whole day chopping down trees and cutting them up.

Behind these beasts of burden the sky was turning mother-of-pearl; delicate pinks, creams and a rich gold. The sea took on the same hues, until a dark pink spread over it like oil.

A girl aged about eight, in the remains of a dress, and with a stack of wood on her head, summoned the energy and the goodwill, apparently effortlessly, to give me a smile of pure delight, and to wave as she passed. When I waved back she almost ran to catch up with her exhausted father, and chattered to him excitedly about the foreigner.

The sky turned scarlet; it was on fire, and the swallows screeched as they sped low over the breakers' pink spray.

'What do you do?'

'Business.'

The man was drinking tea with us in the centre of Teknaf. We'd got down, slightly shaken, from the bus, and dived straight into the nearest place of refreshment, where this half-Bengali, half-Burmese businessman had engaged us in conversation. In fact he'd strolled over from another tea shop in order to join us.

'What kind of business?' I pressed.

He looked embarrassed, and glanced around the shack, as though he might find an answer among the biscuit jars, or in the tea kettle boiling in the clay fire. His friends, and everyone else in the place laughed, until he came up with, 'Well, you know, Burma's quite near.'

There was no need to add that in Burma the people are short of everything, that the country which once kept half the subcontinent supplied with rice now imports it, that consumer goods fetch high prices, and that the River Naf is a permeable border.

Teknaf felt like the end of the earth. In a way it is. Situated at the bottom of a long spit, with the River Naf on one side and the sea on the other, it's isolated geographically, even if it is the centre of a big smuggling operation. But then most of rural Bangladesh is isolated, and Teknaf is lucky to have a road – a semi-tarmacked track which isn't motorable during or after the monsoon, when the pot-holes turn into hippo-sized mud baths.

'Where are you staying?' It was the smuggler-businessman again.

'The Water Board's bungalow.'

Three Burmese monks in scarlet robes, carrying scarlet paper sunshades greeted an old woman in the tea shop, and sat to indulge themselves on tea and biscuits.

'You should stay at the Forest Department bungalow,' said the smuggler.

'Yes, we might, if we catch the Sub-Divisional Forest Officer. He's supposed to be there with his family now. How far is it from here?'

'A five *taka* rickshaw ride.'

The rickshaw driver wouldn't take less than twelve *taka* from us, and as we rode out of the town towards the Forest Department's bungalow a four-wheel drive Mitsubishi land cruiser passed us going the other way. An overfed family glanced disdainfully at us – two grubby, travel-stained foreigners – through its tinted windows.

The vehicle had contained the SDFO and his family, but at the bungalow two men were drinking tea on the veranda and one told us that it didn't matter – we could stay anyway. They were representatives of two distinct types: a dark, fat one who talked as though addressing a rally of thousands, and a tall, younger city type – an educated man who considered himself above rural living. The city type seemed unhappy about allowing us to stay but the first one shouted for the servant, who introduced himself as Hanif.

As I unpacked I heard them arguing about us on the veranda.

'Why let them stay? It's only more work for Hanif.' – the city type.

'Yes,' came Hanif's reply, 'but it *is* my work. Don't you understand? This is what I am supposed to do. It's more interesting when there is work than when there's no one here.'

The two Forest Department officials had gone by the time we'd washed and changed, and Hanif brought us tea on the veranda of the bungalow. He also brought a guest book for us to sign – the one slim volume went back to 1958. I leafed through it: one guest, a retired civil servant, had written that he'd last stayed in 1943, and was pleased to find it unchanged, and a recent visitor reported 'a wild elephant in the jungle up behind the house'.

I asked Hanif about tigers.

'No there aren't any really. Only small ones.'

'Only small ones? What's a small tiger?'

He laughed and shrugged, disappearing back to his house a little distance away, where his wife remained shut up inside all day, and all night. Islam is strict in these remote areas.

The bungalow was built of wood and split bamboo, but to a standard,

74

colonial design: steps leading onto a veranda, from which three sets of double doors led to bedrooms on either side and a dining room in the middle. Each bedroom had its own bathroom – a basin, a shower and a bucket, which Hanif filled from the well outside (neither the taps nor showers worked). At the back was a small kitchen. For some reason the whole place was painted silver inside – to keep away mosquitoes or flies perhaps.

The veranda looked out over the River Naf, barely ten yards away. On the far shore, a mile distant, rose the hills of Arakan in Burma.

We stayed on the veranda for the rest of the afternoon and evening, drinking a concoction Peter created from smuggled Chinese gin (which he'd acquired in Teknaf little more than three minutes after alighting from the bus), and freshly squeezed lime juice. We also tried it with green coconut juice, but it wasn't as good.

The full moon rose in the cusp of the mountains across the river, which was dotted with the sleek, low fishing boats of the south. It hung there, a luminous globe suspended over the river, flooding the smooth water with quicksilver. Occasionally we saw lights signalling across the river – smugglers arranging a rendezvous perhaps – and the dark jungles of the far shore seemed full of mysteries.

Or so I thought until Peter, after a long, contemplative silence, said that it reminded him of Lymington.

His voice came from somewhere deep within the embrace of a planter's chair – a kind of wood and cane affair designed for maximum horizontal comfort after a hard day riding an elephant around the forest.

'Nonsense. Nothing could look less like Lymington.'

'Yes it does –'

The plop of oars interrupted him, and a boat crept by below us.

'It looks just like the Isle of Wight from Lymington.'

How he arrived at this conclusion I've no idea, but it was a line he maintained for the rest of our stay in Teknaf.

From beyond the veranda came the noise of a million frogs, geckos and cicadas, and mosquitoes buzzed in our ears. As the tide crept in the waves broke gently on the muddy bank. Occasionally a truck went by, shattering the rhythm of these sounds, silencing them until my ears retuned, or the creatures got their courage back.

'Perhaps the smuggler would arrange for us to be taken to the Isle of Wight in one of his boats,' I suggested.

'Let's see if we can go legally first.'

We'd heard that there was some local deal going whereby people could cross the river into Burma without visas, as long as they didn't stay longer than twenty-four hours.

'No, no, that's only for Bangladeshis with relatives on the other side,' laughed the local Bangladesh Border Rifles' commander when I asked about it the next day. I'd gone into town to get some breakfast – Peter was still asleep, suffering from the after-effects of Chinese gin – and seeing the military outpost, painted red and white, on the edge of the river, I'd gone over. The commander was a dapper little man, with a combed moustache, and he talked to me at the gates of the base – I wasn't allowed in. 'There wouldn't be any problem as far as we're concerned, but the Burmese would go wild. They'd probably put you away for years.'

The businessman-smuggler wasn't any more optimistic, 'You could go in one of my boats,' he said after I'd tracked him down and we'd drunk a cup of tea together. 'But it's more of a risk for everyone ...'

I suggested that we could pay for the trouble caused, but the more he thought about it the less enthusiastic he grew. 'The Burmese are pretty trigger-happy, you know, and with elections coming up they're very suspicious. You wouldn't get far before you were stopped.'

He'd convinced me.

We were sitting in a tea shop, and several children had already stopped to ask whether I was going to the beach. They seemed excited about something so I decided to follow them, although the only explanation I got from the smuggler was a shrug and one dismissive word, 'Fishing.'

Walking along a sand path between paddy fields and areca nut plantations the first sight was a boy carrying a snake-like knife-fish (as they're known locally), which was bigger than he was, straining to hold its head above his shoulder, while its tail dragged in the dust.

The closer I got the more children I met, and they all carried fish: fish in baskets, in plastic bags, on their heads, threaded on string in ones, twos, threes, by the dozen, long ones, thin ones, fat ones, fierce ones and funny-coloured ones.

Everyone had fish on the brain that day for the conjunction of a full moon, a high tide and mild weather had brought the shoals in, as it did every year at this time, and the town was taking advantage of it.

On the beach, the southern end of the seventy-mile stretch from Cox Bazaar, the scene was more like a religious festival than a fishing event. There were perhaps a thousand people, all wildly excited, milling about, gathering in groups, dividing, shoaling and working together. The jeeps screamed onto the beach, skidded across the wet sand, through the crowds, and pulled up facing away from the sea in front of one of the newly-landed catches. The fish were unceremoniously shovelled into the back of the jeep until it was full to the tops of the seats. Then they'd drive off again, crazily, at breakneck speed.

The white beach stretched away in both directions, fading into spray in the north, below steep, sandy cliffs topped by jungle. Along the line of the tide lay shells of all shapes and sizes, starfish and jellyfish. A man offered me three enormous crayfish for a hundred *taka* (after a month of bargaining practice I was able to tell him confidently that it was too much), and another approached with a basket of black and red tiger prawns. But all this was peripheral.

It took me some time to figure out exactly what was happening, so great was the confusion. The fishermen took a drift net out by boat, crashing their heavy wooden craft through the surf by brute force, and circled round until the net was fully extended. To each end of the net was attached a large rope, held by a group on the beach, who slowly and steadily hauled the net in. This took nearly an hour, but once it was close to the shore everyone joined in; up to a hundred people formed a barrier, holding up the edge of the net, to prevent the fish from leaping out. These precautions weren't enough for some fishermen who set up a second net behind the first to catch the knife-fish which leapt, silver arrows, over the raised walls of their cage. Other fishermen grabbed at the air with their bare hands, catching fish in mid-flight and flinging them violently back into the whirlpool of white water, eyes and fins which surged within the ever-decreasing space.

At last the net was pulled into the shallow water, and the heaving, sliding, jumping silver mass quickly slackened and dulled in the midday sun, which dried the salt like streaks of white blood on the fishermen's dark faces. Then the knife-fish, the most valuable, were sorted from the rest, pulled from the net – they had identified their enemy – which they gripped with half-inch, curved teeth. One man showed me where he'd had a chunk of flesh snapped from his calf by one of these predators. The remainder, *pfasha*, a kind of sardine after which the predators come, pomfret, and many unidentifiable monsters, were sorted less carefully, although the fishermen kept an eye out for a tiger-striped ray with a black-and-white whip of a tail. If they found one they picked it out gingerly, and flung it far out to sea.

Around the edges of this excitement ran the children, hundreds of them, stealing handfuls of flapping silver wherever they could, stuffing the things into plastic bags, into their lungis or their skirts, making only the vaguest attempt to hide what they were doing, or to wait until the fishermen were distracted by something else. For the most part their thieving was tolerated, or ignored. Fish were so plentiful that no one bothered about how many went missing; in six hours I saw only two fishermen lash out in anger, or curse and throw a handful of sand at a child. It was a hopeless task trying to prevent the kids anyway – they were too nimble, and there were too many of them. Most of the fishermen seemed to take the attitude that each child could only carry so much, and afterwards there'd still be plenty for everyone.

As the light faded the men gathered their nets onto strong bamboo poles and carried them inshore, to be stored until the next day, and I started back to the bungalow, carrying three crayfish. The moon rose yellow into an angry red sky which had turned the sea pink: a primeval sunset. The fishermen stumbled along beside me, caked in salt and exhausted by their efforts. In the fields people were gathering piles of dried fish onto mats, and among the smooth stems of the areca nut trees lamps flickered like fireflies.

The smell of fish filled the air.

This was poverty-struck Bangladesh!

The road back to the bungalow, with the river on one side and the steeply rising jungle on the other, was puddled with warm and cold air; walking it was like swimming across a deep lake, with some of that fear of creatures which might rise up out of the dark.

I scrambled up into the jungle, past an enormous acacia beneath which a family was husking their rice crop on the concrete-hard ground. A man whipped two bullocks round in a tight circle, keeping the halter pulled close, while behind him his wife and daughter spread the rice sheaves. They'd bound pieces of cloth around their heads, to cover everything but their eyes, against the dust which rose and hung golden under the tree.

Two teenage boys who'd been lounging under the tree watching the husking nudged each other as I went past, and got up to follow.

The path was steep, and I pulled myself up by hanging onto roots and branches. At the top it flattened out and the ridges stretched away, running in parallel lines to the north, covered in green. Where I stood most of the big trees had been cut down a long time ago, but further away they towered over the hills, gigantic mahoganies and teaks, like geysers gushing from the earth.

The two boys stayed ten yards distant, and we played a game. I turned down a side track, hoping to lose them, and they waited for me to come back, knowing that it was a dead end; I loitered until they had to pass, or acknowledge that they were following me, and they stopped to admire the scenery.

Finally I asked what they wanted.

But they didn't want anything. They were going for a walk, they said, innocently surprised by my anger.

At the top of the hill were the remains of two Buddhist stupas. The sun-baked bricks were spread out over a wide area; they hadn't crumbled from neglect, and I thought they'd probably been pulled down. It had happened some time ago – small trees and plants grew up through the tumbled bricks – perhaps twenty years before, at the time of Liberation from Pakistan.

The boys too peered at the bricks, and sat when I sat in the shade to look out over the river, towards Burma. They stood too when I stood, and followed me further into the jungle. I forced them to go past me, doubled back and took another path. They could have found me easily, but perhaps they'd understood because I didn't see them again.

The path followed the top of the narrow ridge. It snaked in and out through the trees and roots, and after twenty minutes I stopped in a glade to rest. It was humid despite the shadow of the trees, and I wanted to listen to whatever sounds there might be. I sat on a convenient tree root, polished smooth through long use as a seat, and waited for my ears to pick out the different noises.

The first and most obvious was that of chopping, of *dao* (machetes) methodically cutting wood, then voices, laughter and an occasional snatch of song, but these were distant, and through them came the softer, more subtle voice of the jungle: a million insects making a million different buzzes and whirrs, the noise rising in obedience to the commands of some invisible conductor, and then falling again; the rustle of leaf on leaf, shaken by a sea-breeze; the monotonous screech of a brain fever bird which mounted in pitch, and ended in a series of sharp stabbing sobs, before starting all over again.

Four boys, their lungis tied up between their legs, and one girl, came into the clearing and put down their loads of wood, resting them upright against a tree-trunk. None of the boys was old enough to shave but they were as well built and as strong as men, while the girl was at least as strong, if not stronger than they were. They threw themselves down on the earth, and one told the others that Peter had taken his photograph yesterday. It was a boast, and the others were impressed. They wondered whether we were Muslims, how old we were, and what we were doing, but this discussion was of limited interest and they soon started teasing the girl.

It was rough talk; they had no pretensions to education or culture, and no fear of a distant god who might punish them for some little understood sin. One of the boys and the girl were in love, which made them cruder and more direct in their jokes about one another, but they also made eyes and touched – not gently because their friends were watching. There was a physical spark between them which they couldn't resist. Of course the others knew it, and a comment about pigs rubbing up against each other brought the girl to her feet with a *dao* in her hand. She wasn't going to use it, she wasn't seriously offended, but she did extract an apology, or an explanation of sorts, amid much ribald laughter.

After that they changed the subject. They joked about the man who bought their wood, and how he told them that the price had fallen if they brought in a big load. They seemed to find it genuinely amusing that he cheated them and thought that they didn't realize. They were what educated Bengalis call 'simple people', unsuspicious and easily used.

A family who'd been cutting wood for themselves came into the clearing, silent under the gaze of the professionals: a man, a teenage girl and a small boy.

'Let's see what the Buddhists have got,' one of the woodcutters said, and they all lounged back to glare.

The man strained under a bundle of sticks, which they didn't count as a load.

'Oh, well done uncle, very good,' laughed one. 'Careful you don't break your back.'

The man's daughter was so exhausted that she put her wood down to rest, despite the taunts. One of the woodcutters spotted that she was holding some wild bananas. He pointed at the tiny, five-fingered bunches, widely separated on the stem, and laughed at her for taking them. He grabbed them off her, and took a couple of bananas to inspect more closely. He peeled one with his *dao*, and gave it to me. It was less than two inches long and consisted of many black seeds held together by a thin coating of banana. It was pretty to look at, but so bitter to the taste that I had to spit it out.

The Buddhist girl cried, and the woodcutter, perhaps ashamed of his bullying, returned the rest of the bananas, helped her balance the wood on her head, and told her to go carefully.

Then it was time for them to leave also. The men shouldered their sixty- or seventy-kilo loads, with difficulty, and much flexing of hard muscle. It took two of them to lift the young woman's stack of logs onto her head, and when she was helpless, straining under the weight, her neck muscles bulging, they poked her a little in the ribs, just for the fun of it. She tried to smile, but it came out as a grimace, and she lifted her *dao* in a silent threat before setting off down the path, followed by the others.

The boats to St Martin's Island were said to leave at 9.00 a.m. We got there at the right time but there were no boats. Someone said that one would arrive from the island soon. Others disagreed, saying that there would be no boat from St Martin's but that one would leave for the island at 11.00 a.m., or midday. Another told us that there would be no boat that day, but many the next.

After waiting four hours we went for a swim in a man-made pond full of red water lotus surrounded by tall palms. Nearby a boy shinned up an areca nut tree. When he was clinging on at the top, next to the bunch of pods, another boy came and started to push the thin trunk. It was easy to make it sway, and soon the boy at the top, forty or fifty feet up, was describing an arc – six or seven feet one way and six or seven the other. He clung on for dear life, until his friend grew bored with the game and stopped.

A boat was about to leave when we returned to the jetty, and we clambered in along with a spare propellor shaft, chickens, sacks of rice, tins of biscuits, buckets of betel leaves. It was a small boat and it wasn't easy to find a comfortable position among all these goods and the twelve other passengers.

We chugged out of the creek and into the River Naf itself before the water ebbed too far, and stopped twenty yards off shore. The anchor was dropped. A boy clambered out, swam ashore and disappeared. There was no explanation and I couldn't understand the replies to my questions.

The boat swung in the current, and I inspected the other passengers, several of whom seemed to belong to the category of what Jamaicans classify as 'small island syndrome'. I wondered whether going to St Martin's was such a good idea after all. The man beside me was a good example. He wore an old astrakhan hat, squashed down over a low forehead, his features were twisted and mean, and he regarded everything with suspicion.

An hour passed in this limbo – despite the time of day the sun was still hot. The conversation flagged, everyone was tired, and no one knew how long we might have to wait. A note was passed to us from the stern. It read, in English: 'Please give your boat fare two hundred *taka* (2 persons) plus two hundred *taka* return fare. Thank you'.

Peter laughed and threw it overboard, knowing that the fare was about fifteen *taka*, and that there was no such thing as a return fare.

Another half hour went by, and the boy returned carrying a bunch of areca nuts and a packet of biscuits. That was it.

It was dark before we were out of the estuary, breasting the waves which broke over the river water flooding into the Bay of Bengal. Before the moon came up we were out in the darkness, with only the flash of the island's lighthouse, twelve miles away, to guide us. The sea marked our passage with phosphorescence, which seemed to reflect the Milky Way above, brighter and clearer than I'd ever seen it.

We were going to St Martin's, I reminded myself, because it was the furthest point south, and because all Bangladesh is made up of islands like it. Virtually every village is an island to itself, relatively recently cleared of jungle and settled. The first settlers went to an uninhabited St Martin's less than a hundred years ago. They exist, Bangladesh's villages, in semi-isolation and self-sufficiency, with their own words for things, their own customs and ideas. Villagers' knowledge of the outside world comes from travelling singers, talk in the weekly bazaar, and from the rare person who returns from the big city. It's a circumscribed, limited life, and I hoped that St Martin's would be a good example.

The boat scraped on the beach, and we jumped down into darkness, into thigh-deep water, carrying our bags. The beach was a minefield of boats and anchors, to say nothing of ropes, and once we'd successfully negotiated these we made for the only light we could see – the other passengers had disappeared – and stumbled into a tea shop made of split bamboo with rough tables and benches set in the sand.

The proprietor told us that the only place to stay was the house of the local political leader, who was known grandly as 'the Member' (of the local Union Council). He turned out to be a tall man with a full white beard. He was watching a black and white television, powered by a car battery, or rather he wasn't watching it – he was switching manically between the Bangladeshi, Burmese and Indian channels, although this last was little more than a blur and a buzz. It came down to a choice between a good, clear picture of a Burmese general making an exhortatory speech, but without sound, or Bangladesh TV's snowed-out offering of The Cosby Show (in English and incomprehensible anyway).

As far as the Member was concerned it was a close-run thing, but he sensibly decided that a Burmese leader waving his arms and mouthing great rhetoric was of marginally greater interest than the noisy Cosby Show.

He was then free to turn his attention to the two foreigners who'd been unexpectedly washed up on the shores of his island. The problem, we discovered, was that it was harvest time and his spare room was occupied by the labourers imported from the mainland to do the work. However, he hospitably turned them out onto the veranda, and we were given their accommodation – some smoothish wooden planks nailed loosely to a bed-frame, no mattress and no coverlet.

There was no question of our refusing this inequitable arrangement, of saying that we'd prefer to sleep on the veranda. Our arguments were met with blank incomprehension. As far as they – the Member, his family and the labourers – were concerned, we were causing trouble. We ran the risk of offending them, of conveying the impression that we expected something better.

We gave in, and slept fitfully on the boards until 5.30 a.m., when the household started about its business.

The Member had built his house in a sandy coconut grove, and the mature trees kept the place shaded and cool. Like many country places everything had been carefully thought out, and was in its place – a clay storage pot, big enough to hold a child, under one tree contained fresh water. Half a polished coconut shell floated on the surface, for use as a scoop. Nearby was a tubewell, with a square, cement surround, for washing. Beside the path leading up to the house was a stone-lined pond with fish and white lillies. Steps led down into it, and to stop people falling in at night a fishing net had been tied between the coconut palms. It wasn't very effective, and the local Muslim priest caused much amusement by falling in that night. On the other side of the path lay a stack of unwinnowed grain, also netted off, to prevent the chickens from stealing it.

There were children everywhere, playing hide and seek, and chasing each other through the trees. They could more or less understand my Bengali, and I them, but when I tried to talk to the Member's first wife, an enormous and proud lady, who looked like a Rakhine, we discovered we were mutually incomprehensible. The Member had ten or so children by three wives. The second two were kept well hidden. It was difficult to find out precisely how many children there were as each person I asked gave a different answer, and perhaps no one had bothered to count them all up.

Some of the children were inbred and odd, and one, the first wife's youngest daughter, was a sad sight. She was ten years old, and she lay on the veranda all day, unable to move or speak recognizable words. At night she was carried inside, where she slept on the floor of the room Peter and I had been given. The other children said that the girl was mad, that it had happened suddenly a few years ago. Her mother was the only one who bothered to communicate with her, and they seemed to have a real rapport. The girl's head was shaved, and she stared at everything which went on around her with enormous dark eyes, until with a despairing groan she would turn her face to the wall and close her eyes.

I told the girl's mother via one of the other children about a hospital in Dhaka which specializes in paralysis, and which gives treatment for free. She did seem interested, and I said that if she wrote, someone would come from the hospital to see whether they could treat her daughter. But she was illiterate, how could she write a letter? she asked. Her husband wouldn't do it, and anyway Dhaka was too distant a place for her to think about.

Once we'd talked to the fishermen laying out fish to dry on racks along the beach, and been told that the island sent nearly a thousand tons of dried fish to the mainland every year, we'd just about used up all sources of entertainment. The only thing left was a walk round the island, but we'd gone little more than five hundred yards when we were stopped by an army officer dressed in a lungi and a khaki shirt, open to his midriff. Shaving soap stuck to his face. Our unexpected appearance had evidently put him in a bad mood.

'Who are you? Where are you going? What are you doing?' he demanded aggressively. 'How did you get here and when did you arrive? Where are you staying?'

We answered his questions, and he calmed down sufficiently to invite us into the Bangladesh Border Defence Rifles' camp. A path, marked out from the sand with alternating, freshly painted, red and white pebbles, led through a cactus hedge to a couple of tin huts, a radio mast and a flag pole. Nearby was the cyclone shelter, built on concrete piles, twenty feet up in the air, and we sat in the shade beneath it. I was introduced to the radio operator, and tea and biscuits were brought. The army officer, a major, became quite friendly, and we even exchanged addresses. There was much they wanted to know, such as the difference between London and England, whether Stockholm was in London, and what exactly was meant by 'free sex'.

I asked whether any tourists ever came to St Martin's.

'Yes, yes, every year thousands come.'

'Thousands!'

'Yes, thousands.'

He liked being based on the island, he said, and his life was easy, although he did leap up once, spilling his tea, and rushed down to the beach, shouting at a boat which had anchored offshore. It was high drama, and the fishermen stopped mending their nets to watch, in a neutral way. He waved his stick, and sent the boat away again, minus one unfortunate man who'd made the mistake of alighting from the boat. The officer whacked him across the shoulders a couple of times with his stick, and abused him, and a soldier led him a way to the lock-up.

'The boat was from Burma,' the officer said when he returned from doing his duty. He unbuttoned his shirt again. 'They are smugglers.'

'What will you do with the man?'

'He will be questioned.'

'And then?'

He was at a loss, but only for a moment. 'Then ... then we'll get to the bottom of the matter.' He smiled triumphantly and looked pleased with himself.

When I asked about it in the village later on I was told that the officer would take a small bribe and release the man, whether he really was a smuggler or not. It happened all the time.

The south end of the island, beyond which there was nothing, was a bleak salt swamp. Some kind of yucca tree thrived and the beach was covered in sharp coral boulders. The contemporary rubbish consisted of one, or rather half, a flip-flop, washed up among the tropical flotsam – otherwise there were only coconuts, a turtle shell, a smashed fishing boat, and the spiked armour and skeleton of a pufferfish. Everything was bleached white against white sand so when I saw what I took to be a long piece of green and yellow rubber I reached out – until it backed up and hissed at me, turning into a snake.

'It's not dangerous,' said a boy airily – he'd appeared out of nowhere – tossing a handful of sand at the evil-looking thing. But I noticed that he didn't get too close.

'Unless it bites you,' I suggested.

'Even if it bites someone he won't die,' he told me over his shoulder, as he walked purposefully off along the beach, his destination as mysterious as his sudden arrival.

The trouble with the uttermost ends of the earth, in Colin Thubron's felicitous phrase, is that when you get there you find that it's small and there's not much to do.

Boats returning to the mainland, to Teknaf, were as difficult to find as they had been going the other way.

The engine of the one we did catch broke down at midday. We drifted slowly towards Burma and grilled in the sun while the owner chatted unconcernedly to the passengers. The approach of rocks and a cliff face, against which the breakers sent up plumes of spray, seemed to discomfit no one, with the exception of Peter and myself. At what point does one jump? we wondered.

The owner didn't condescend to fiddle with the recalcitrant engine – his only tools a spanner, a piece of bent wire, and an oily rag – until, after an hour, his assistant had failed to fix the problem. His intervention proved effective, and we were denied the opportunity of an unexpected landfall in Burma by a choking roar from the engine. Clouds of black smoke engulfed us and we set off once again in the general direction of Teknaf.

8

Into the Hill Tracts

Kasem knocked on the hotel bedroom door back in Cox Bazaar, and when I opened it I recognized the tiny sparrow of a man from the description I'd been given: the only person who could take us into the Hill Tracts. Friends had been ambivalent about him, but I'd been unable to understand exactly what the problem was.

Our conversation went something like this.

'Me Kasem. Going.'

'Come in, sit down. Would you like some tea?'

'Telling. Going Lama Para.'

I pulled out a chair and he sat down. 'Tea?' I asked, trying to speak clearly.

'Cox Bazaar much walking. Military camp Lama. No good.' On the table in front of us was a sheet of paper, he pulled it towards him and sketched a rough map. 'No good. Stopped me taking.' He put his wrists together as though handcuffed, and his skeletal face split into a wide grin.

'Japanese bombing,' he continued, 'boom, boom, much bombing, gun for aeroplanes there by pagoda temple. Deaf making. Me Moulmein going. Wartime. British army me. Sixty-five me. Nigeria going.'

He tapped a hearing device beneath his black waistcoat, twisted the thing in his ear, and pulled gently on the wire connecting the two.

'What?' I asked, overwhelmed by this incomprehensible stream of information.

He ignored the question, or failed to hear. It was hard to tell with Kasem, and a week later I was no nearer knowing. He adjusted a pair of horn-rimmed spectacles which dwarfed his impish face, and pulled a blue scarf more tightly round his scrawny neck. His left shirt sleeve was rolled up, but the right one was held in place by a cuff link. I guessed he had only one.

'Speaking African language. Nigeria going. Me taking National Geographic Magazine 1971. Picture. Me all languages speaking, Mru language, Chakma language, Burma language. All, all me showing. My picture taking. You me going one Mru village, one Tippra village.'

'How many days will we need?'

'Yes, yes, Mru. Going.' He smiled beatifically at me. 'Me two houses. Here Cox Bazaar one house five children, me another house six children in forest. Mru wife. Me very friends with Mru. Thirty-five years me guide. Know all. Burma going, Assam going. Not now, now bad.'

'How much?'

'Yes, me very friends. Headman my friend,' he replied pleasantly, doodling with the pen.

'How much?' I screamed at him in Bengali.

Perhaps my red face suggested what it was I wanted to know, although it seems unlikely – he was as thick-skinned as a rhino – in any event he put one hand inside his waistcoat to twiddle the volume control of his infernal machine.

'You me?'

'And a friend.' Peter was out.

'Friends, yes you me.' My pocket-knife caught his eye, and he picked it up. 'Good knife. France knife.'

'Yes France. But there will be THREE of us.' I held up three fingers and switched to Bengali, 'I have a friend.'

'Two people? You Bengali speak. Good. Easy.'

In fact it wasn't any easier as he still couldn't hear and he spoke Bengali in the same abbreviated, pidgin way that he spoke English. I grabbed the knife off him and put it down the other end of the table.

'Two, yes.' I shouted.

'Three friends?'

'No! Two!'

'Two people going for ten days.' He doodled on the paper, and eventually wrote a dollar sign and a number with several noughts after it. 'Guide fee.'

Peter came swinging into the room at that moment. I didn't try to introduce them but gestured at Kasem. 'You have a go. It's not easy. That figure he's written is the fee he's suggesting for ten days in the Hill Tracts.'

I leant back in the chair and closed my eyes, listening to Peter's attempts at communication, trying to hold back my laughter.

'I see,' he said after a minute. 'It's a bit one way isn't it? The hearing aid doesn't make any difference? Shouldn't think it works.'

And on cue Kasem said, 'Batteries. Not possible good batteries in

Bangladesh. You have batteries for camera. Give me.'

In the interests of international understanding Peter handed over a couple of his valuable camera batteries. They made little or no difference.

Haggling is never easy, but it can be fun. It wasn't with Kasem, but after some time we arrived at a more reasonable, and mutually acceptable sum. He sighed as though we were cheating him, and talked about how much he liked English people. 'Special price, English only. Like English people. Very kind generous people.'

In view of the difference between his initial demand and the price we actually agreed (in *taka* not dollars) this can't have reflected his feelings. Then, without warning, he was off again, chattering about elephants, tigers, jungle and 'much hilly', and tapping his old legs. He seemed pleased, but announced, just as I thought he might leave, 'Permission needing. Tomorrow going army. Permission giving. All coming.'

'What permission? No one will give us permission.'

'Yes, yes, permission.' He gave me his pen. 'You writing. "To Director Tourism Cox Bazaar. Asking for going Lama. Very kind permission asking." Your names giving. Me guide writing. Writing. Then both signing.'

I translated this into English as best I could, but there was more. 'Presents bringing,' he said, and indicated that I was to take further dictation. 'Writing then buying,' he ordered peremptorily. 'One hundred cheroots, twenty-four bangles, twelve mirrors, twenty-four combs, much colours buying. Girls and boys long hair, liking colour, looking bright, bright, smiling.' He mimed the actions of someone combing their hair and looking at themselves in a hand mirror.

'Good cigarette lighter for headman. Two kilos sweets needing for children. Also bringing five kilos rice, one kilo onions, spices, garlic, one kilo sugar, tea, powdered milk . . .'

I was beginning to feel that he had employed us, or rather me, as a scribe. We celebrated after Kasem had gone by finding our way to an illegal bar beneath one of the big Rakhine houses. It was like being beneath a ship: full of enormous black tree-trunks supporting the beams and wide planks of the house above. Everything was spotlessly clean, even the underside of the floor. We sat on a park bench which had somehow ended up there and the woman of the house brought us a jam jar of alcohol and two glasses. The husband, in a black Burmese lungi, paced up and down the garden in a thoughtful sort of way, as though he'd been relegated there by the women – who were having a riotous time above us. Once or twice I caught a black eye regarding us through a crack in the floorboards –

one of the younger girls, the older ones were far too poised and dignified to stare at anyone, especially not a foreigner.

We were three quarters of the way through the third jam jar when a splendid old lady was led across the yard by one of the breathtaking teenage daughters. She was dressed traditionally in black, with a silver belt, and sported an impressive array of gold teeth. At the bottom of the stairs leading into the house she stopped and stared me straight in the eye in a rather severe way. She was no more than three feet away and didn't look terribly friendly, so I put my palms together in front of my face and said, 'Namushkar.'

The old lady smiled, probably in response to my foolish grin, and greeted me in return, 'Namushkar.' She held my gaze for a moment then went up the stairs on her granddaughter's arm nodding and laughing to herself, and repeating, 'English, laughing, laughing, good, good.'

Kasem turned up punctually at the arranged time the next morning. The by now depressingly familiar sound of someone testing a microphone burst across the lake in front of the hotel, followed a short time later by the usual hectoring, abusive scream. The politician, or prospective politician (it was always a man), bullied his audience, and I could only think that if I had the right to vote in Bangladesh I'd refuse out of principle – who'd want to be governed by someone who could behave like that even before they'd been elected?

We still didn't understand where we were going – I knew that there was no one who could give us permission to enter the Hill Tracts apart from President Ershad himself or the General Officer Commanding Chittagong – and neither was in Cox Bazaar that day. When Kasem deigned to semi-comprehend our questions he gave no useful information, and conversation was so impossibly wearing that I'd come to accept this as a mystery tour. After a short walk Kasem ushered us into an enormous, air-conditioned and carpeted office in the Tourist Board. A fit-looking man finished signing a couple of letters then stood, shook our hands, said how pleased he was to meet us, and took the letter which Kasem had dictated the previous day.

The final version read, 'We would like to seek permission to employ as our guide Mr Kasem for a trip to Lama Para. We will depart from and return to Cox Bazaar.'

Kasem hovered in the background, playing dumb.

On the walls were expensive blown-up photographs of Cox Bazaar and St Martin's Island, neatly labelled in the military manner.

The man looked up from the letter. 'You're from London?'

I nodded.

'Both of you?'

Peter woke out of his daze and said yes.

'Why do you want to go to Lama? A week is a long time. There's not much to do there.'

For some reason Peter launched into an elaborate story about how his stomach was acting up. He's normally pretty silent, but this yarn went on and on. He wanted to walk slowly, he said, that was why we were planning a long trip. At which point I kicked him as we weren't supposed to be walking anywhere; there was a bus to Lama Para, and we had to pretend we were going to take that. He ignored me, certain that he'd come up with a convincing argument.

The man listened patiently, waiting for Peter to wind down, then delivered a body blow, 'If you have a stomach complaint then it's best not to travel at all.' Perhaps it was my imagination but he seemed to stifle a smirk. 'The food isn't good in Lama, nor is the water. Yes, by far the best thing would be if you stayed here.'

He folded the letter into a square.

Another, fatter man entered the room, without knocking. He took the letter and glanced through it. 'Actually,' he said, 'we may not be able to spare Kasem. Someone may want him as a guide.'

'But we want him as a guide.'

He nodded thoughtfully, as though he'd consider it, and the first man reminded the newcomer that as Kasem wasn't a real employee of the Tourist Board they had no control over where he went or what he did.

Both of them turned on Kasem, who was hanging about near the door, apologetically, as though afraid. It was clear to me that he was acting. He had no respect for these two pompous men, but they were powerful, and his way of dealing with power was to feign fear, to cringe. Their questions were direct and to the point, but Kasem wound them up by not hearing, misunderstanding and answering different questions. It was a tactic which worked, for the men quickly lost their tempers, shouted and abandoned all hope of a sensible discussion. They dismissed him as a fool, although he was playing a far cleverer game than they were. They turned wearily back to us.

I felt the first glimmerings of respect for Kasem then.

'Actually,' the first man said, 'I have no competence in this matter. Permission must be sought from the competent authorities. As far as we are concerned any tourist can go anywhere in Bangladesh, but the proper authorities must be asked.'

To show willing I wondered whether we should ask the military.

Neither of the two men batted an eyelid, but they agreed that this would be the right course of action. The interview appeared to be over. As far as I could see we'd achieved nothing, but when we came out Kasem was elated. He shook our hands and jumped up and down.

'Permission. Yes, yes. Permission. We have now going.'

'What permission Kasem? They didn't say anything. They said we should go and ask the military.'

'These people military. This one Captain Ifzal. Other one army also. Permission giving.'

This wasn't my interpretation of what had happened, and I tried to ask him if we now had to go to the military base to request permission. His hearing aid stopped working immediately.

'Yes Japanese bombing, boom, boom, boom. Up there, big gun. Aeroplanes . . .'

'What about the military?'

'Mru people. Going one village here,' he sketched a wide arc with one arm. 'Then another one. Then Tippra village. Mru my very friends.'

I shouted then, but he was determined not to understand.

'Water no good.'

I interrupted and held his arm, rather too hard, while I screamed into the infernal machine hidden in his waistcoat pocket. He responded sulkily by saying that we could go to see the military if we wanted.

'Is it necessary?'

'Not necessary. Now cigar buying. Come.'

It seemed easier to go along with him than to attempt further questions – he'd beaten us, just as he'd beaten the two men. 'Those people knowing nothing. That Captain Ifzal. Pictures on wall not St Martin's Island, Kasem knowing, not St Martin's. Other place. But writing St Martin's. Stupid people.'

The house he took us to smelt richly of tobacco. In the dark interior four women rolled thick cigars, and cracked jokes about us in Burmese. We bought a hundred for just over a pound. It was worth it for the packet alone, which conveyed the following information: 'Diamond Brand Burmese Cigars are Manufatured out of the best quality Tobacco. The Tobacco is specially selected and the particle of dust carefully removed. They are fine blend with natural flavour and taste. Relious and pleasant to smoke. Cigar Smokers will appreciate the flavour of the Diamond Brand Burmese Cigars.'

'No talking anyone,' Kasem told us on the bus. 'Somebody asking where going, no telling.'

The fact that he was the only person in any position to say where we were going seemed to have escaped him. As far as we knew we were heading for Lama Para, a town in the Hill Tracts, but how we were to get from there to the villages he'd mentioned, or where they were, was an enigma. It even crossed my mind that Kasem had no idea what he was doing, that he'd successfully conned us into giving him a large amount of money, and that he might disappear at any moment. Our difficulties were compounded by the lack of detailed, large-scale maps of Bangladesh. Almost the only one available is a US Airforce map which marks disused wartime airfields, useful if the Japanese have invaded Burma and you're planning to bomb them, but no towns or villages.

The bus dropped us in the middle of nowhere twenty miles north of Cox Bazaar. It was midday, my rucksack was heavy with food and gifts, and Kasem had been arguing with some rickshaw drivers under a tree by the side of the road for a good fifteen minutes.

'Hello, my good friend. I am a teacher in the school here. Perhaps you are going to the Hill Tracts?' The man stood at my elbow, and peered at me through thick glasses.

I muttered something incomprehensible.

'It is not allowed.' He paused. 'You are Englishmen, from Great Britain?'

I replied in French, which usually floored persistent questioners, although Peter had been caught out the day before by a Bengali who spoke it fluently.

The teacher wasn't to be put off so easily. 'In the Hill Tracts there is much danger. Perhaps you are going to Lama Para? You are journalists I think.'

This happened to us throughout Bangladesh. Peter, with his camera bag and hard-bitten, travelled look, was a give-away, but those we needed to convince of our innocence never doubted that we were what we said – tourists, travelling around the country for no particular reason. We got used to illiterate peasants shouting, 'Hey! *Sangbadik*!' (journalist) to attract our attention. But army officers, policemen and government officials, the people who mattered, fortunately believed what we told them, rather than the evidence of their eyes.

Kasem had concluded negotiations with the rickshaw drivers, and I waved to the teacher as we rode off down a brick path, overshadowed by bamboo, towards the hills. He watched us go with a puzzled frown.

The ride was rough as at least thirty per cent of the bricks had been stolen, and I was grateful when it came to an end half an hour later in front of a wide, shallow river, the Matamurhee, which flows from the Hill Tracts. The land was beginning to get hilly, although we were still a long way from the jungle.

Peter and I sat in a particularly squalid tea shop while Kasem negotiated for a boat which, he said, would take us most of the way to Lama Para.

The news that two foreigners had arrived spread through the village in no time, and within a few minutes the tea shop was heaving with men who'd come to inspect us. They were too polite to stare openly, but they assumed that we had no language in common, and didn't want to buy tea, so there was an uncomfortable, shifting silence, broken only by the owner who tried, without success, to take commercial advantage of the sudden rush on seats in his establishment.

'Tea?' he asked each new arrival hopefully. 'A biscuit?' He sighed resignedly at the shaken heads, as though he knew it was a hopeless task but he had to try. He was the only person among the fifty or so crowded into the place who was uninterested by our presence. He stared out across the dusty street toward the hills, nibbling dreamily at a biscuit.

The boat Kasem organized was operated by a man and a boy, who punted us along efficiently. We lay in the shade under a curved cane roof, and made desultory conversation with a sleepy man who was on his way to the market a few miles up stream, a place called Manipuri Bazaar, where people came down from the hills to trade with people from the plains. Or so we were told – Kasem wouldn't allow us to get out and look.

'Way back looking,' he said. 'First going Hill Tracts, then stopping. Army in market. No looking now.'

Many other boats were drawn up on a sandbank near Manipuri Bazaar. Sacks of rice, dried fish and baskets of vegetables were unloaded, portered through the shallow water and manhandled up the steep bank below the market. Three pretty Bengali girls stepped daintily into a dinghy and were rowed across. They stood unsteadily upright, clinging onto one another, giggling and nearly overturning the boat, but determined not to dirty their fresh white clothes by sitting. Peter raised his camera and they pretended to hide their faces, but managed to ensure, that their amused, sparkling eyes, at least, were visible.

After twenty minutes we set off again. Lama Para was four hours away – it would be dark by the time we arrived – and we settled ourselves into the soporific rhythm of the boatmen's punting. The boy, balanced with one foot higher than the other on the wide bow, made from a single trunk, rocked back on his heels, pushed the pole firmly down and leant forward on his toes. He looked as though he could have continued forever.

The river slid by like a green mirror, ocasionally shattered by the electric blue flash of a kingfisher, and an explosion of metallic droplets.

The Hill Tracts are made up of a number of ridges which run north-south and are, in effect, the western foothills of the Chin Hills in Burma, the highest point of which is Mount Victoria, at ten thousand feet. Between the ridges are low-lying valleys. The Matamurhee River runs northwards, parallel to the hills until it reaches Lama, then turns abruptly west. It cuts through the first line of ridges, and meanders across the plain to the Bay of Bengal beyond.

A couple of hours after leaving Manipuri Bazaar Kasem announced that we were going to stop and walk.

'Walk to Lama from here?' I asked foolishly, forgetting Kasem's disability. 'Why?'

He replied succinctly for once, 'Yes.' That was all the information we could get out of him, and he set off into the hinterland jauntily, carrying his shoes over his shoulder. 'Good idea. Kasem good idea,' he said to himself happily.

We plunged down into shallow valleys, where tiny rice fields competed for space with streams, up over hillocks, and past a couple of small settlements. We met one person, an old woman, whom Kasem greeted with pleasure, and they talked for some time in the Chittagong dialect.

'Yes, yes, very good,' he announced when they'd finished. 'No problem. We go in. No problem. This very important woman. Headman's wife. She saying no problem. If problem us no going. If angry people cutting heads. She say no problem. We going.'

Peter tried for more details. 'Where Kasem? Where are we going? Going village? Going Lama? Where?' He pointed, turned his palms up, shrugged and looked questioning – a series of gestures which he's employed with success on the wildest and woolliest of Tibetans.

Kasem remained impenetrably protected by his hearing aid. 'Hungry? Eating?' he enquired pleasantly.

There were moments during the next few days when our guide was fortunate to escape strangulation. This was one of them.

We followed him blindly, having neither a choice, nor an idea about where we were going. The path led up a hillside near a newly built road going to Lama. In the recent past there were only two roads in the Hill Tracts, but with assistance from generous and thoughtless foreign governments wide tarmacked roads have been built, so the army now has direct access to most of the area. The phenomenal cost of these switch-back roads is cynically justified as development of the area for the sake of 'the backward tribal people'. In fact, wherever the roads have gone Bengali settlers have followed, and with the protection of the army they've stolen the tribal peoples' land.

We crossed the road and continued up a steep hill opposite. Behind us a vehicle ground round the hairpin bends. Peter and I ducked behind a small bush as the green, camouflaged truck full of soldiers came into view. Kasem marched on up the hill unconcerned, but it seemed better to be on the safe side, even if we did feel foolish cowering behind bushes and generally behaving like boy scouts.

The path led up and up, and the vegetation became denser, although it was largely secondary growth. In front, as we breasted the hill, the higher ridges of the Hill Tracts, of Mizoram in India, and of Arakan in Burma came into view. The Matamurhee valley was spread below us. Its rice fields and villages were lost in deep shadow, although we stood in the warm glow of the setting sun.

The path wound down, over and round the ridge, through real jungle. Kasem pointed to the roofs of a village hidden among the trees a mile away, 'There going. Before dark coming.' He was excited at the prospect of arriving at a village, and turned his dark eyes, magnified through his thick lenses on us, 'Girls not like Bengali girls,' he said, and tittered, 'very big strong.' He thrust out his pitifully thin chest, making himself look all the more like a sparrow after a dust bath. But he was tired from our walk, and in reality he was past such strenuous effort. His days of leading people through the jungle were over. He limped and was often unsure of his footing, although he put a brave face on it.

The sound of women's voices carried up to us, and Kasem shouted something, a greeting or a question. There was a shocked silence until he shouted again, then laughter and below us we saw three women with great loads of bamboo on their heads scurrying down the path towards the village. They seemed eager to escape from us, or Kasem, rather than to greet him despite his constantly repeated assertion that all the tribal people in the area knew him well and liked him. 'Everyone know Kasem,' he'd say, 'everybody liking. Me knowing girls since babies. Me uncle.'

Sugar Daddy would have been a more accurate term.

The Mru had chosen a spectacular place to build their village. The twenty houses overlooked a deep, overgrown valley, and were perched on the top of the ridge. The valley was scored with marks of erosion, where the monsoon rains had ripped trees out of the earth and left jagged red scars through the green forest. The annual rainfall in this area approaches that of the wettest place in the world, Cherrapunji, a couple of hundred miles to the north, which records an average of forty feet a year. The Mru have learnt to cope with this by building their houses on bamboo stilts lashed together in a complicated arrangement like scaffolding.

The Hill Tracts is bamboo country, and I can't improve on Captain Lewin's description, written a hundred and twenty years ago. In his book, *Wild Races of South Eastern India*, Lewin, who became one of the most sympathetic and knowledgable of the British Chittagong Hill Tracts' Commissioners, wrote of the tribal people:

> The bamboo is literally his staff of life. He builds his house of the bamboo, he fertilizes his fields with its ashes; of its stem he makes vessels in which to carry water; with two bits of bamboo he can produce fire; its succulent young shoots provide a dainty dinner dish; and he weaves his sleeping mat of fine slips thereof. The instruments with which his women weave their cotton are of bamboo. He makes drinking cups of it, and his head at night rests on a bamboo pillow; his forts are built of it; he catches fish, makes baskets and stools, and thatches his house with the help of the bamboo. He smokes from a pipe of bamboo; and from bamboo ashes he obtains potash. Finally his funeral pile is lighted with bamboo.

The headman's house, where we were to stay, was entered via a log with rough steps cut into it, and the hill on which the house was built sloped so steeply that its outer wall was at least twenty feet up in the air.

News of our, or Kasem's arrival spread quickly, and as it grew dark the house filled with young people from the village. We lay on the split bamboo floor, beside the fire in the airy interior of the grand house, surrounded by twenty inquisitive teenage boys and girls, and watched Kasem distribute the presents we'd brought.

He started with the cigars. Everybody wanted a cigar, or two or three, and many teased Kasem, complaining loudly that he hadn't given them one, making him part with another. People came from outside to collect their dues: cigars, sweets and combs, and then they lay on the floor asking questions. At first they tried to question us through Kasem, but his deafness frustrated them as much as it did us, and we learnt our first word, of the Mru language: *na-pang*, stone deaf.

The young men and women lay close to one another, touching and joking. Around the girls' upper arms were tight bands of silver, the muscles bulged on either side, and in their ears silver cones. They wore short black skirts, split on one side to the top, held in place with thick silver belts. Their legs and torsos were bare.

There was a story about the skirts the women wear. A long time ago a certain queen noticed with regret that the men of the nation were losing their love for women, and were more attracted to other men. The queen determined to stop this and promulgated a rigorous order, prescribing the form of skirt to be worn by all women in the future, and directing that the men should be tattooed in order that by thus disfiguring the males, and adding piquancy to the beauty of the women, the former might once more return to the feet of their wives.

The story made sense, especially in the half-darkness; it was difficult to tell the difference between the sexes, for both were extremely handsome and both wore their hair long, tied up in knots, and decorated with coloured combs. On balance the boys seemed vainer, and pampered themselves more than did the girls, although there was no doubting their fitness and strength. Both boys and girls had the physique and grace of natural athletes, of people whose lives were spent in physical labour, and who had the diet, the calorie intake, to support such a strenuous existence – unlike the majority of Bangladeshi peasants.

The boys' games were rough. The firelight flickered across their broad backs and muscled limbs, and they fought each other in sheer enjoyment of their strength. They laughed at Kasem and rolled on the floor clutching each other in delight when he fell into some linguistic trap they'd laid. They soon got bored with his deafness though and switched their attention to a great pile of flowers dumped among them by the headman's wife. They sorted through the pile carefully, choosing those which most pleased them for their colour, or scent or shape, and helped one another to adorn themselves. They made neat bouquets and pushed them through the holes in their ears, or into their glossy black hair, then sat back to admire one another.

One fourteen- or fifteen-year-old boy came in for particular attention from the girls. His name was Lung Wohr, and he was by far the prettiest of them. Kasem laughed at the way the girls brushed his hair, and held his head in their laps. 'Girls wanting young men for marriage. Always marrying younger man,' he explained. He gestured at the headman's daughters, 'These girls older, maybe eighteen. Taking boy for husband soon.'

He stroked the shoulder of the girl sitting nearest to him, and she jerked away, shivering in horror at being touched by this ugly old man whose skin hung loosely and whose body had none of the taut, healthy glow of

Lung Wohr. Kasem seemed oblivious to the girls' disgust of him, or chose to ignore it; he was forever touching and stroking them like animals, and they did all they could to avoid him. His attitude in general was patronizing and he behaved as though the Mru were dangerous animals which had to be placated or calmed with gestures and gifts, as though they could be tame if treated properly, but that they retained the potential for savagery.

In fact their responses were more complex and sophisticated than his.

Kasem had obviously never read Captain Lewin, who noted that he had found

among all wild and so-called barbarous races that when one grows acquainted with their language, and they, becoming habituated to you, allow a knowledge of their social life and habits, they are very much the same as other people; there is not much difference, indeed, between human nature all the world over – they love and hate, eat and drink, live and die, in much the same way, and often in a far more natural and sensible manner than we of the civilized races, who hold ourselves so loftily aloof in our fancied intellectual and moral superiority.

Kasem was upset that I'd bought the wrong kind of sweets to give as presents to the children. He claimed, with exaggerated fearfulness, that if the children weren't happy then no one would be happy, and then, he insisted, 'Very danger ... head cutting. Mru people most dangerous people.'

A less likely scenario than the one he described was hard to imagine – the children were, of course, delighted with what we'd brought. Throughout our stay in the Hill Tracts however, Kasem insisted that it was only his diplomatic skills and knowledge of the local customs which preserved our lives.

The trouble with sleeping on a bamboo floor is that it's like a trampoline, so when the headman's wife started to move about at dawn, to rekindle the fire, we were all bounced awake. The Mru don't wake up quickly though; it's a slow, gentle process, not a matter of a quick cup of coffee and then off to work.

As the dark thinned out and the sun lit first the tops of the trees on the hillside opposite, then worked its way down until it struck into the village itself, another fire was kindled outside. People stood around it in a companionable sort of silence, gathering themselves for the day, the women in red woollen shawls. A man, the priest of the Mru religion, held someone else's baby, and played a complicated musical instrument, looking a little like a set of bagpipes – with a large gourd instead of a bag – but sounding like a number of different flutes. The high, clear tune echoed out across the valley, as though calling the sun down on us.

It was decided that we would follow the headman's daughters to the family's *jhum*, the plot they'd cleared in the jungle for cultivation. The two determined and purposeful girls, dressed in their finery of silver, flowers from the previous evening and red cloaks, had already shouldered cane baskets and headed off for the *jhum*, taking about a kilo of cooked rice each, wrapped in a banana leaf.

We were accompanied by a man called Chongbot, who led the way out of the village as people drifted away to do their tasks for the day – the headman to chop wood or cut bamboos, his wife, carrying a headbasket full of gourds with fresh leaf stoppers, to collect water from the stream at the bottom of the hill, and others to renew and repair their houses.

The path went up over the next two or three ridges, and plunged down again, in places so steeply that tree trunks with steps cut in them had been propped upright, to act as ladders. Around us a flowering creeper had covered whole trees, smothered the ground, and crept up bamboos, bending them over with its weight, forcing them into green arches from which flashed the scarlet fire of its flowers.

We tried to find out from Kasem how far the next village was, and how long it would take us to reach it the next day. He determinedly misunderstood us, and Chongbot laughed at our attempts to communicate, 'Kasem *na-pang*,' Kasem's deaf, he repeated.

We ended up high on a hillside where the *jhum*-house had been built like a look-out post, with views over the width of the Lama valley hundreds of feet below. It was on stilts, with a veranda, like all Mru houses. In the distance was the next ridge, and beyond it two or three more. Beyond them, I knew, lay Chapa Tong and the seven-thousand-foot Blue Mountain in Mizoram. There were flowers everywhere, the path up to the *jhum*-house was lined on either side for a hundred yards with plants resembling marigold, astilbe, lemon balm, and other herbs and sweet smelling blossoms. I picked one and put it in my wallet. It's still there, its fragrance almost as strong now as it was six months ago. The girls filled their baskets, supported on straps around their foreheads, with hill cotton and returned to the *jhum*-house for lunch.

They poured the cotton onto the veranda and crashed into the one room – less clumsily than myself who managed to put a foot through the bamboo floor. I hadn't yet learnt to keep an eye out for the weak spots in the floors, and avoid them. The girls tut-tutted, but Lung Wohr was unintimidated and he jumped up and down, making everything bounce –

girls, food, baskets, the white pumpkins which littered the place and even
the fire. They pretended to be annoyed with him, but were too busy to
keep it up. They didn't stop working for a moment. One lit the fire,
another made a spoon from a bamboo in a matter of seconds and used it
to eviscerate a pumpkin or two, a third opened their packets of rice and
a basket of black freshwater crabs. The crabs were already cooked and
they ate them greedily as they waited for the vegetables to boil. They bit
off and spat out the head and poisonous lungs, then cracked open the
shells with their fingers and sucked out the meat.

A kilo of cooked rice would have floored me, but they swallowed it
with relish, and looked ready for more, kneeling forward over their banana
leaf plates and smacking their lips, pictures of rude good health. After
eating they brushed out their long hair, retied it in buns, and sorted out
a selection of flowers, replacing those from the previous night with fresh
ones. Lung Wohr sprawled amongst them, making them laugh with a
constant stream of chatter, and allowing them to pamper him. He was in
fact rather prettier and more delicate than they were.

Only then did Chongbot let us know that he spoke Bengali, and I asked
him about the Shanti Bahini, the tribal guerrilla army which is fighting
the Bangladesh military in the north.

'We don't like them, and they don't come here any more. About ten
years ago they used to come and demand money, rice, chickens, all sorts
of things. Every month they'd want something, and they'd even take
whatever woman they wanted. The army couldn't do anything about
them.

'In fact the soldiers were afraid, they didn't like to go into the jungle
because they always got killed. But we were able to push the Shanti Bahini
out of the area.'

Kasem, who'd been listening, nudged me, drew a finger across his
throat and then pointed at Chongbot, 'Very danger,' he said, looking
serious, 'but with Kasem you OK.'

Chongbot ignored him. 'Now, all our problems are with the Bengali
settlers. The army doesn't give us too much trouble, but the settlers! They
come to the village area and cut down our trees and our bamboo. We
need bamboo, we make everything from it. They cut it down as though
the forest belonged to them, or to no one. If we remonstrate with them
they ignore us. They steal our chickens, our rice, anything they can get
hold of. In the space of six years Lama has become a Bengali town. It
used to be a tribal town, but now you don't see a tribal anywhere.'

Chongbot's hair was chopped short, unlike the other men in the village, and I asked him why he didn't wear it long.

'It's too much trouble. This is more modern,' he replied shortly, but when I pursued the question he admitted that the real reason was different. 'If we go to Lama, to the market, with long hair people look at us and think we're savages from the jungle, so they try to cheat us. Also it makes you stand out. The soldiers are more suspicious of tribals who keep their hair long, and you tend to get dragged in for questioning even if you've only been to the market. So why put up with it?'

The more I learnt about the village and its problems the more convinced I became that their way of life was finished, even if they didn't realize it yet themselves. The people of the village, Chongbot, Lung Wohr, the strong girls and the children would end up like those Chakma at the northern end of the Hill Tracts: dispossessed, terrorized refugees dependent on the so-called goodwill of a government which doesn't respect them. Then it would be too late for them to fight.

It's easy for governments to ensure the impoverishment of indigenous people, and then claim aid (easily misappropriated) from the West, from the World Bank, the United Nations, or the Asian Development Bank, on their behalf.

The government isn't the only problem the Mru has to put up with. That night, back at the headman's house, the talk was of bears, tigers and missionaries (which they seemed to equate). Kasem said that at the American-run Dulodara Christian Memorial Hospital near Cox Bazaar they were all spies. No one cared much for the missionaries even though all tribals who go to the mission hospital receive free medicine, clothes and even money if they want it.

The headman put it succinctly, 'We are Mru. We have our religion, so why do they come here to bother us?'

There was a deaf mute among the group and he wanted to get back to the subject of wild animals; he acted out how he was once attacked by a tiger, but survived because his wife buried her *dao* in the creature's skull. This was clearly an old story, and everyone had seen the dramatic mime many times before. They agreed that the only truly dangerous animal was the bear, and they made one unfortunate young man repeat his story several times. They found it hilariously funny, and rolled around on the floor clutching their sides as he told it.

Chongbot was laughing so much that I couldn't get him to give me more than an abbreviated translation.

'I was out chopping wood, and as I walked home I found a bear cub, so I picked it up.' This was the point at which everyone fell about – the young man should have known better than to pick up a bear cub. 'I was going to bring it home, but I'd only gone about half a mile when the cub's mother rushed out of the jungle. I was so frightened that I dropped the wood I was carrying, threw down the cub and ran for it.'

The description of his abject terror, and the action of throwing down the cub, brought tears to the eyes of the audience, and they made him re-enact the final bit of the story two or three times.

'There's only one thing which will stop an angry bear.' It was the headman again. 'A bullet between the eyes. And it has to be from an army rifle, a good one. A *dao* is no good, no matter how much you chop at a bear's face or arms it carries on.'

I tried to tell a story of being chased up a tree by a rhino in Nepal, but no one knew what a rhino was, so although they got the general idea – large animal, me running and climbing – and laughed, it fell a bit flat, and anyway the deaf mute had again engaged people's attention. He mimed how he'd once come across a bear with its head down a hollow tree trunk, guzzling honey. Behind it were three or four cubs which tapped their mother to remind her that they too liked honey. Occasionally, with her head still buried, she'd pass a clawful back to them. 'So,' the mime was translated for me, 'I joined the cubs, tapping and pulling at the mother's fur, and ate a bellyfull of honey before going on my way.'

Unlikely as this story sounded no one cast any doubt on it, although Chongbot did suggest that the man was crazy for taking such a risk.

An old man who'd been watching quietly from a corner suddenly spoke. 'Pretty man?' he asked in English, pointing at Peter.

I was startled. 'Pretty!'

'You pretty man. He pretty man?'

It wasn't an adjective which anyone had thought to apply to either of us before, and it seemed unlikely that the man intended to flatter us.

'Pretty?' he asked again.

I was at a loss as to what he could mean, and being unwilling to agree tried to change the subject. 'Where English learning?'

'Pretty Army. Japanese fight,' he said promptly.

Everything became clear. 'Yes, we're both British, pretty, I mean.'

He was a quiet, kind old man, and at Kasem's insistence he agreed to accompany us the next day to another village a few miles away, as did Chongbot. Kasem, it turned out, didn't know the way.

9

The Trap

The first mile or two was easy enough. We followed a path up and down steep hillsides, past old *jhum* fields overgrown with the fiery, flowering creeper, then down into a steep-sided river valley. After that the route ceased to exist, it became more like a steeplechase without horses. Since the road has been built the small footpaths which used to crisscross the area have fallen out of use, and we followed the bed of a stream.

I was ill prepared; my sandals stuck in the mud and my feet slipped twice at every step – once in the sandal and once on the mud. I quickly decided to abandon them, but the mud was full of sharp stones and twigs so I made slow progress in comparison with Peter, who had boots, or Chongbot and the old man whose soles were hard as leather. Only Kasem was slower, and although he kept saying that this was the kind of walking he liked he was struggling to keep up.

We followed the stream for miles, going along what resembled a dark tunnel, water beneath our feet, rock walls on either side, and an impenetrable mass of trees and ferns above.

The next stage involved us in a struggle up a sheer, sandy incline overgrown with thorny and stinging plants. It took almost an hour to reach the top, where there was a *jhum*-house and a path which would take us straight to our destination. Chongbot was most disgruntled at having to take such a difficult route when there was a perfectly good road to walk along, and it dawned on me that he thought we had permission to be in the Hill Tracts. Later, when he knew, I asked whether he'd take us further and deeper into the area, up to the Burmese border, or northwards towards Bandarban. He was tempted by the idea I could see, but after some thought he said simply, 'If you get permission I'll take you anywhere. Just come back when you have a permit and we'll go travelling for a month.'

Peter and I discussed the possibility of heading off by ourselves endlessly, deciding that the only way to do it would be to follow the old

footpaths along the tops of the north-south ridges. The river was out –
Kasem had informed us that the army searched all boats which came up
the Matamurhee – and the valleys were too thickly populated with Bengali
settlers. But it would be a difficult journey, without proper maps or a
guide, through territory we didn't know, and as we weren't equipped for
such an adventure it would necessitate returning to Cox Bazaar first. There
were also other dangers which we were unaware of until later the next
day, and one convinced us that we'd kill ourselves if we tried to go it
alone.

We rested at the top of the incline and I noticed that Peter's calf was
bleeding profusely, turning his sock red. 'You've been attacked by a
leech,' I told him cheerily, pointing at the stream of blood. 'It's dropped
off now.'

He swore and sat down to search for more of the horrible creatures in
his boots, and the rest of us examined our legs and arms carefully. Peter
found several in his boots, gorging themselves, but I was free of the things
and reminded him that the Bengali for leech is *joke*. Comparative linguistics
doesn't usually attract so much rancour, but it might have been wiser not
to have made this observation.

The Mru village we arrived at an hour later was less isolated than the
first one, and neither Peter nor myself felt comfortable there. For a start
the house where we were told we'd stay seemed poor, although we were
wrong about this. There were also two Bengali traders in the village,
buying ginger from the Mru. They were offering a third of the price it
fetched in the Chittagong market. One, a man with a badly smallpox-
scarred face and a blue scarf tied round his head as though he had
toothache, was particularly unpleasant. He marched into the house where
we sat drinking tea and recovering from our walk and started to question
Kasem; Are they American? Are they missionaries from Dulodara? What
are they doing here? Where have you come from today? and so on. He
didn't get any answers, but none of the Mru had thought to interrogate
us in this way, and we were in their village.

By the pond at the bottom of the hill below the village, Chongbot said
a prayer to the spirit of the pool, or the water, before he'd allow us to
wash, but he dismissed a bamboo shrine nearby as 'Bad'. Of course I
questioned him more closely, but he wouldn't go beyond the statement
that it was something to do with 'Shaitan', or the devil.

'Actually,' Kasem said, having recovered his hearing sufficiently to
know what we were talking about, 'actually the Mru have no religion.'

Chongbot and I ignored him, and we poured libations of cool, clear water over ourselves from the gourds provided. Kasem had been gettting worse over the past twenty-four hours. Not only did he order any and all Mru around as though he had a natural right to their attention – Chongbot was already carrying Kasem's bag – but he didn't even do it with good humour. Sometimes they ignored him and his commands, but more often they obeyed with a grim smile, perhaps because this was how all Bengalis treated them.

As we climbed back up the hill we were treated to the sight of the smallpox-scarred Bengali trader literally dragging a young Mru man away by the arm, insisting that the boy carry the load of ginger that he'd managed to rob someone of.

The house where we were put up had a floor made of teak planks a yard wide, rather than of bamboo, and contained a chair, although everyone sat on the floor. On the wall was an election poster which encouraged people to vote for, to place their mark next to, Man Kong Mru's symbol – a cup of tea – a symbol of wealth and luxury. The owner of the house, Man Kong Mru, was a politician and businessman. He wasn't there but his wife moved about quietly, carrying their small son, playing with and teasing him. She ignored both us and the men who crowded into her house to feed their curiosity in the evening, but helped Kasem prepare a meal of mashed, rehydrated rotten fish (a great delicacy), and green chillies – in about equal proportions.

At one point Kasem told everyone to go home as Peter and I wanted to go to sleep, although we'd said no such thing. Fortunately no one took any notice of him. Everyone was waiting for Man Kong Mru to return; they wanted to see how he'd react to the unexpected arrival of two foreigners.

When he came he was drunk, not falling over drunk but enough to be noticeable. He was a small man with the bullish look of Edward G. Robinson, and he dominated the room from the moment he entered. Whereas his wife, and all the other villagers were traditionally dressed, Man Kong had short hair, and was wearing trousers and a jacket.

It was easy to see why the government had nominated him as a local political leader. He wasn't impressed or taken in by Kasem's over-the-top compliments on his fame and greatness, and kept interrupting with, 'OK, OK, what else? Get a move on.' Finally he tired of the game and started to ask us direct questions.

The clincher came when he wanted to know whether we were Christians. This was easy, and we denied it emphatically, throwing in that we didn't care for missionaries, or 'machineries' as Kasem called them, either.

Man Kong eyed us suspiciously and threw a fifty *taka* note in the direction of his wife, ordering her to fetch a bottle of rice spirit. 'See,' he said, 'I even pay my wife for the alcohol she brews. You are my guests and we must drink.'

When it came he slammed the bottle down in front of us, then filled three glasses to the brim.

If his intention was to test whether or not we were 'machineries' we passed easily; the brew was tasty, with no fire to it. But we'd polished off the bottle between the three of us before things began to relax.

'You buy another bottle,' Man Kong ordered. 'Give money to my wife.'

He was drunker now, and a more commanding presence for it. He'd lost interest in us, except as audience to a display of power. The second bottle came and he pulled several pieces of paper from his pockets, telling Kasem to read them out to the assembled villagers (and us). They were letters which gave him the contract to extract stones from the riverbed, for road building. It was a massive contract, worth perhaps a million *taka*, and I began to see in him something of the stereotypical self-made man and local politican. Arrogant, clever and noisy, a good manager of people, and one who believed he'd got there by his own efforts, by his own intelligence and hard work alone. He wasn't someone who felt that he owed anyone for anything.

I wanted to ask whether he'd been given the stone contract for agreeing to stand in the elections, and so running the risk of being shot by the Shanti Bahini as a traitor, but it's not the kind of question you can ask of your host. At least not in that situation – I was already worried that he'd go straight to the army the next day and report us.

Man Kong hadn't been elected of course, and Chongbot laughed at my naïvety when I asked; a Bengali settler had been declared the winner.

'Do you want to see some Mru dancing? I'll arrange it all for you tomorrow. Do you want to see it?' Man Kong asked.

I'd drunk too much to be careful, and despite an elbow in the ribs from Peter, who'd been stung in this way by Arab village chiefs and Tibetan wide-boys before, was sufficiently non-commital for Man Kong to inter-pret it as a positive response.

We then had to spend fifteen minutes persuading him that we didn't have a thousand *taka* to blow on such an event, and anyway weren't interested in a show put on for our entertainment alone.

He was most disgruntled. 'It's nothing,' he told the assembled village men, to most of whom a thousand *taka* represented a good month's

107

income. He regarded it as miserliness on our part, unable to understand our unwillingness to watch a dance put on for our benefit alone, divorced from any mystical or religious meaning, with no purpose other than that of separating us from our money.

When Man Kong shouted for a third bottle of spirit his wife remarked that he'd had enough, that we'd all had enough, and went to bed – without fetching another bottle. This caused some unease among the assembled men, reminded perhaps that their own wives might be ready with some sharp comment about being out late and drinking too much when they got home. They drifted off in ones and twos, shaking our hands and smiling broadly.

Kasem and Chongbot were sent to sleep in another house.

Man Kong hadn't finished with us though. He perhaps feared us, or feared our presence. Perhaps he thought we'd come to assassinate him, or he was just playing safe. Feigning greater drunkenness than was justified by the amount he'd consumed, or was indicated by his conversation, he stumbled over to our bags, stacked in a corner, and started to pull out our things. The only items which delayed him were Peter's collapsible camera stand, which did look as though it might be a weapon of some kind, and his Japanese head-torch.

Man Kong demanded a demonstration of how the camera stand worked, and once satisfied turned his attention to the torch. He was fascinated by it, attached it to his head, to his arm, even a leg, and paraded around the room laughing, much impressed by the practicality of the Japanese.

'You won't keep that long,' I muttered as I turned in, leaving Peter and Man Kong to fight over possession of the gadget.

'Want to bet?'

An hour later I was woken by their laughter – they were still amusing each other by thinking up different uses for the torch – but I'd under-estimated Peter's tenacity, for it was back in his bag the next morning.

The big event of the morning was Man Kong's present to his son: a pair of red and white plastic shoes which squeaked at every step. To tell the truth these amused us and his father more than they amused the three year old, who had acquired a pet in the form of a large black beetle, on which he doted. Man Kong's wife had attached a string around the beetle's thorax, and the boy gripped this leash as though he had a tiger on the other end, dragging the unfortunate insect around in the dust. However, we soon understood why he held on so tightly. In a last-ditch attempt to escape, and with a thundering whirr, the beetle launched itself into the air like an overloaded cargo plane. Held in check by the string it whizzed round and round the boy's head for several minutes until, realizing its impotence, it folded its wings and crashed to the ground like a Kamakaze pilot.

What with the squeaking shoes, the furiously buzzing beetle and our hilarity, it was a noisy morning.

The difference between the two gifts seemed important to me; they symbolized the dilemma faced by the Mru, and by other tribal peoples in the Hill Tracts. On the one hand the modern, artificial world by which Mru culture and society will be overwhelmed, or become a deracinated tourist attraction, and on the other traditional Mru society. Either way the space allotted to them is diminishing, and within a few years their choice will be between fleeing Bangladesh or submitting to the impoverishment of their society, culture and life.

Man Kong had already chosen, and was clever enough to profit from it.

After we'd left the village and were walking past the cliff we'd scaled the previous day, I asked Chongbot whether he'd ever been to Cox Bazaar.

'Yes, I like it, but it's not as good as Chittagong.'

'You've been there too?'

'Once only, but it's a great city.'

'Why is it better than Cox Bazaar?'

'There are fewer trees and hills. Yes, it's not like the village. Here there are too many trees. In the city it's all concrete and big buildings. The fewer trees, the better I like it.'

I began to see his point when we plunged into secondary jungle, an area which had been *jhum*-ed by his village twenty years before, but which was now overgrown. Razor-sharp bamboo leaves sliced our arms and faces as we progressed in single file behind Chongbot, who widened the path with his *dao*. We were following a pig track, he said, that was why it was clear underfoot and to thigh level. Progress was slow, and we talked little, saving our energy for the steep climbs and sudden descents through this wilderness. After a couple of hours we heard laughter and found ourselves looking down, though an enormous bamboo stand, onto a *jhum* where two women worked, filling their baskets with cotton, I dived into the bamboo thicket ahead of Chongbot, but he gripped my shoulder so hard that I cried out. He pulled me back, out of the bamboos, and wouldn't let go until he was sure I'd got the point – that I wasn't to go that way.

'Look,' he said, pointing deep into the undergrowth before us.

I could see nothing. It all looked the same to me, and I had no idea what I was supposed to be looking for. A wild boar ready to charge? A tiger? 'What?' I asked, rubbing my shoulder.

'There. Look carefully. Beside the pig track.'

The bare earth which marked the track went almost straight ahead, through the bamboos and into the top of the *jhum*. Shadows fell in all directions, confused further by the shimmer of bamboo leaves disturbed by a breeze. I followed the line of his pointing finger, and saw what? A piece of cut bamboo lying horizontally through the stand. A large bamboo, perhaps two inches in diameter, had been split in half and cut to a four-foot length. It came to a sharp point, like a stake, and it lay a couple of feet above the ground, beside the path. As I stared I saw that there were more of these stakes further along, that the thicket was seeded with them.

'Trap.' Chongbot informed me. 'Look.'

He chopped a branch from a nearby tree, trimmed off the twigs and leaves, and pushed it down the track towards the stake. There was a loud report, a crack, and with the hiss of an oiled machine the first stake shot across the path, burying its point in a tree on the other side. The bamboo stand shook as though in the grip of some wild animal.

'A booby-trap, yes, I see. Shall we go another way?'

Chongbot laughed. 'Pig-trap. Sometimes we set the whole lot to go off at once because pigs go around in families: boar, then mother pig, then the baby pigs, in single file. So we get them all in one go.'

He retrieved the spear and with a couple of swipes with his *dao* brought the point to needle sharpness again. Motioning us to keep well out of the way he reset the trap, using all his strength to pull back the ten-foot bamboo spring which projected the missile. It was a complicated and finely balanced system, but it was set in motion by a simple trip-wire. 'We used the same technique against the Shanti Bahini,' he informed us conversationally.

I shivered, not so much at my escape, but at the sheer brutal efficiency of the thing.

Chongbot talked as we circled the bamboo clump. 'If the point goes in just behind the shoulder, it will kill the biggest boar straight away. The difficult thing is to set them at the right height, especially if they're in series. And then it's annoying to have to reset them all if they've gone off and you haven't get anything to show for it.'

'We shouldn't go to the next village today. To get there we'd have to cross the road a few times, and that's where the army is. Why not go tomorrow?'

'Why's it better tomorrow?'

'It's Sunday, and the army doesn't work on Sundays. There won't be anyone on the road, so you can walk there more easily. Spend another day with us, in our village, and leave tomorrow.'

Foolishly, as it turned out, I believed this piece of information, about the army not working on Sundays, but then stranger things are true in Bangladesh.

It was good to be back in Chongbot's village, and we were greeted like long-lost relations, although everyone was fed up with Kasem's penchant for misunderstanding. In response to his constantly repeated, 'Kasem good idea, me good idea', and his bullying manner, even the children had begun to respond with, 'Kasem *na-pang*'.

When Kasem learnt that the headman's elder daughter was to be married soon he sat down next to her. 'You'll die,' he said firmly. 'You'll grow old so quickly. Much better to stay at home. Don't do it.' Leering like the most depraved lecher he tried to stroke her bare shoulder, but she shied away from him. For a man with two wives and two families Kasem was showing himself up as a remarkable hypocrite.

Giving up with the girl he turned to me and launched into a story about his past exploits. This culminated in a description of how, twenty years before, he'd been captured by a tribe of people in northern Burma, Shans perhaps, but his courage, fortitude and strength had saved the day. The story, which went on and on, isn't worth repeating, but *Raiders of the Lost Ark* could have got a few good ideas from him. It was punctuated with monotonous regularity by his catch-phrase, 'Kasem good idea', which heralded yet another remarkable feat by super-brain, Tarzan Kasem.

If he hadn't expected me to believe him, and perhaps he even believed himself, it might have been amusing.

The headman and his wife were going to Lama market so they accompanied us as far as the road. The path led out of the village through bushes and trees warmed by the early sun, and from some invisible, exotic flower came the sweet scent of oranges. We were all in high spirits, with the exception of Kasem who was lost in his own world. As we waited for him to make his way down the last steep slope, muttering to himself, the headman's wife said clearly, in English, 'Kasem no idea!' and laughed – a phrase she'd been saving up perhaps.

Once on the road we said goodbye to the headman and his wife, and set off downhill, three abreast. We'd hardly gone more than a mile when an army jeep came tearing round a corner, overtook us and screeched to a halt. So much for the army not working on Sundays. A lieutenant in the engineers jumped out and strode back to us with a puzzled expression on his face. 'What are you doing here?' he asked sharply.

Kasem was wearing a badge which said 'Tourist Guide', in English, and he replied, 'These are two English tourists and I am working for the Tourism Department.' He tapped his badge. 'We have permission from Captain Ifzal in Cox Bazaar.'

'Where have you been?'

Kasem waved his arm vaguely behind us. 'Just up there.' His hearing had recovered.

'And now?'

'Oh, we're just returning to Cox Bazaar. That's all.'

The lieutenant was in a hurry. He shook his head in disbelief or puzzlement, and reluctantly returned to his jeep. There was something not quite right about this, he knew. As the vehicle shot off again two soldiers sitting in the back grinned and waved to us like schoolboys.

We'd just about recovered from the shock when we rounded another corner in the road and ran straight into a foot patrol made up of a fiercely moustached sergeant major and three soldiers. We stopped. They stopped. The sergeant major came so close he was almost standing on my toes. We looked at each other, and he smiled broadly, 'Anything on my side?' he asked in English, pressing his hands to his chest in a gesture of supplication.

'Charming, charming,' said Peter quietly. 'God knows what he thinks we are.'

We looked, now I came to think about it, like a couple of mercenaries. Neither of us had shaved for days, we both had short hair, our clothes were green and black (tribals are forbidden to possess clothes in these, camouflage, colours), and the three metal legs of Peter's camera stand stuck out of his bag like the barrels of some kind of gun.

I replied with as much authority as I could muster, 'No, I don't think there's anything on your side thank you, sergeant major.'

'Anything, anything I can do I will do,' he added dramatically.

'I'm sure. Yes, very kind of you, but I think we're OK. We'll just ... er ... carry on if that's all right with you ...?'

'Please.' And he stood back to let us pass.

We continued in silence for some time, digesting these encounters. It was clear that meeting foreigners on this road was so unheard of that the patrols had no standing orders. I was thankful that we were in Bangladesh not India, or almost anywhere else. The Chittagong Hill Tracts is a prohibited area. It is illegal, an offence to enter it without the written permission of the General Officer Commanding Chittagong. He's no fool and has never given permission to anyone, except a few journalists who've been ferried about in an army helicopter and forbidden to speak to anyone without the presence of an army officer. In almost any other country in the world we would have been taken away and interrogated by now, and in some we would have been shot out of hand.

We were striding down the road at a good pace, had regained our confidence, and almost believed that we'd make it to the village when we ran into another patrol.

The captain was an older, more experienced man who looked as though he might have been a war hero. His hair and moustache were grey, and he limped badly, dragging his right foot. Behind him were a troop of serious soldiers armed with AK47s and a heavy machine gun of some sort, instead of the usual pre-war Enfield rifles. They spread out on either side of the road when they saw us, and although they kept the barrels pointing down, it wasn't a sight to inspire confidence.

The captain came up to us slowly, sweating profusely in the heat.

'Me no speaking. You speaking,' Kasem whispered hurriedly.

'Where going?' the captain asked in heavily accented English, genuinely puzzled.

I replied as though it were self-evident. 'To Cox Bazaar.'

'Where coming from?'

Trying Kasem's trick I waved vaguely at the hills behind us, 'Near Lama.'

'Lama? You been Lama?'

'Er, not exactly. Close. We've come from a place quite near Lama. We're tourists; we went to the Tourist Board and spoke to Captain Ifzal. He said that as far as he was concerned it was all right if we came up here.'

As I hoped, the captain couldn't follow all of this and he spoke sharply in Bengali to Kasem, but our guide's hearing had inexplicably deteriorated again.

The upshot was that we were marched quarter of a mile back up the road until we came to a hill suitable for radioing base. The captain took Kasem and a couple of soldiers to the top, and politely told us to wait in the shade of a tree at the bottom. Apart from one soldier who stood half-way up the hill, the remainder stayed on the road. Deciding that the time had come to destroy anything which might look suspicious I leafed through my notebook and tore out a couple of pages of Dewey classification numbers – for books from the School of Oriental and African Studies in London. It would be a bore to have to look them up again, but I thought that it might be difficult to convince a soldier, or an intelligence officer that a list of numbers and letters, such as JMFC 307.772 79636, was not a code of some kind.

I screwed the paper into a ball and was tempted to eat it so that I could say I'd done so, but it was a bit large and my mouth was dry; I dropped it down a snake or rat hole at my feet.

At the top of the hill the radio operator was having great difficulty reaching base; there was a lot of crackling and buzzing but not much contact.

The captain, meanwhile, was losing his temper with Kasem – I felt I understood why. 'I know you say you work for the Tourist Board,' I heard him scream in frustration, 'but what are you? A gardener? A peon? What?'

Kasem stayed cool throughout this encounter, and persisted in mis-understanding every word said to him until the very end. He repeated that we were tourists, that we'd employed him to guide us, that he was an officially sanctioned guide, and that we'd been in a village near Lama. He added that I spoke Bengali.

The soldier nearest to us, the one half-way down the hill, turned his back on his officer and smiled at us, 'You speak Bengali?' he asked. 'Where did you learn?'

'I taught English at Chittagong University a few years ago.'

The soldier was impressed. 'You're a Professor then.'

There seemed to be some advantage to be had from this, so lying modestly I admitted that yes, now I was a Professor at London University. At the top of the hill the same misinformation had been elicited from Kasem by the captain, with greater difficulty.

The soldier smiled at us encouragingly as the captain, who clearly would have liked to hit Kasem but didn't dare with us around, shouted in anger at our guide's pig-headed refusal to understand the next question.

'Don't worry,' the soldier said, 'you'll be out of here in no time. It's not a problem.'

'I hope you're right.'

The soldier laughed happily. 'Yes, we'll radio base then a senior officer will arive. He'll talk to you and then let you go.'

It did seem the most likely conclusion, and I wasn't seriously worried. Everything depended on how efficient they were, whether my name was on a file – I've been writing about human rights abuses in the Hill Tracts for ten years.

'Where is your motherland?' he asked.

'England.'

'Is that London?'

'Sort of. Where's your family home?'

'Comilla. It's a nice place. My wife is there and my two sons . . .' Within a few minutes the soldier had given us his family history and a detailed guide to their relative health and wealth.

The captain was shouting into the radio and I was shocked to hear myself described as 'about forty-two', but cheered up when he guessed Peter's age at fifty. He listened to his orders, which were broadcast over half the jungle by the powerful receiver: he was to keep us there, to be polite, to question us thoroughly, and to wait for the major to arrive.

'Bring them up,' he commanded.

We trudged up the steep hill, and when we reached the top the captain smiled as well as he could and shook our hands, as though he'd slipped up when we'd met on the road and he now had to make amends. He was sweating, and for him, of course, this was no game. By contrast we were all right. The worst they could do to us would be to throw us in a lock-up for a few days, give us a hard time and then deport us. As far as he was concerned he was dealing with potential mercenaries, a potential ambush, spies, who knows? Perhaps his foot had been damaged in an ambush. And perhaps this was his area, perhaps he should have encountered us days ago; he may have been worrying about his career.

The captain's questions were random. He had no idea what to ask, or how hard to press, but noted everything down on a scrap of paper with a pen he borrowed from me. Most of the time was taken up with detailing our itinerary since we'd arrived in Bangladesh – where and how long we'd stayed in each place.

We sat on a rubber cape with views in all directions across the hills and the jungle. At times it was a little oppressive to be surrounded by uniformed men armed with powerful weapons, but Peter pointed out that only one of them had an ammunition clip for his AK47. The rest were, in effect, unarmed. No wonder they looked so miserable patrolling the road, and never ventured into the jungle; the foot soldiers were sitting targets. But then there weren't any Shanti Bahini forces in this area, in the south.

I lied about a few things, my name for a start. If there were files and Francis Rolt figured then it seemed silly to give it to them – fortunately my first name's Antony, so I gave that.

The only tricky moment came when the captain asked where we'd stayed in Calcutta. Answering quickly before Peter could pitch us into deep trouble by telling the truth, I said, 'The YMCA wasn't it?' and stared as hard as I could at Peter, trying to make sure he spotted the deliberate mistake.

Kasem was looking most despondent by this time, and seemed to have shrunk to half his already miniature size. He'd switched off his hearing aid completely and wasn't hearing anything. He looked and acted like a deranged old man; his mouth hung open loosely, his hair was all over the place, he had five days' growth of grey stubble, and he stared about vacantly.

If it was an act it was a good one.

Several hours had gone by already, and the major still hadn't arrived. We waited, and the captain tried to engage us in light conversation. We did our best to help him, but we didn't have much in common, and our efforts degenerated into an uneasy silence.

My confidence ebbed when Major Karim did arrive and stepped out of his jeep. He wore dark glasses, was an energetic 35 and maintained an elegant superciliousness. He shook our hands and questioned the captain, who was in a flap about whether or not he'd done the right thing – perhaps he was afraid that we were important in some way he'd missed. Major Karim tried to calm his captain's fears, listened carefully to all that had happened, and then turned to question us. His questioning took the form of a conversation, in English, rather than an interrogation.

'Actually,' the major said, once he'd covered the same ground as the captain, 'actually, we don't allow any foreigners to come here. This is a restricted area. You must understand that it's for your own protection. There has been a little trouble here over the years and the government doesn't want foreigners to be kidnapped. You understand?'

He was very urbane.

'We did get permission from Captain Ifzal in Cox Bazaar.'

'Yes, ex-Captain Ifzal,' he said dryly. 'He's retired. He's not able to refuse or give permission.'

Our apologies for the trouble caused, for the misunderstanding and for being there were waved away.

The major turned towards Kasem, and to my surprise spoke to him politely. 'Now then Kasem, what are you doing here? You know foreigners aren't allowed into the Hill Tracts, so you shouldn't have brought them should you?' He went on in this vein for some time, treating Kasem like a wayward child, as though he was often in scrapes like this.

'I'm sorry,' he continued in English, turning back to Peter and myself, 'for the long time you'll be here.' My heart sank, but he put out his hand

116

and smiled; it was a mistake, he was apologizing for the long time we'd been kept waiting. 'You can go.'

Major Karim took two steps towards his jeep and saw Peter's camera bag – inside were three cameras, a hundred rolls of film, five lenses and a pair of binoculars. He stopped and half-turned. 'Is that a video?'

In Bengali he asked the captain whether he'd searched us.

The poor captain knew he'd made a mistake, but somehow in the heat of the moment he'd forgotten, and he shook his head in the negative, unable to voice the necessary words.

Major Karim stared at our kit and glanced back at us. He was in a serious dilemma; he'd told us we could go, so common courtesy demanded that he allow us to leave without further trouble, but he wanted to know what was in our bags. His internal struggle, and the arguments raging both ways was an almost visible event.

To my amazement politeness won. 'OK. You can go.'

He jumped into his jeep and was gone.

It was too late to go to any more tribal villages, and we weren't in the mood, so we stood by the side of the road and waited an hour or so for a bus to take us to Cox Bazaar. Once there we went to the hotel to pick up the luggage we'd left behind. As usual there were several men hanging around the hotel counter, and when I asked for our luggage one of them muttered in Bengali to the owner, 'Go on, ask them.'

'You've come from Lama?' he asked pleasantly.

There seemed to be no point in denying it. 'Yes. It's a lovely place, we enjoyed the hills and trees and natural beauty very much.'

'And now?'

'Oh, well, we're going to Chittagong on the bus in a few minutes.'

'Have a good trip.'

The plainclothes man left, walking rather faster than normal, and I thought that we'd blown it, that it looked as though we were running, especially as we'd told Major Karim that we'd probably stay a couple more days in Cox Bazaar. But the bus didn't go for another hour and no one came to take us away for further questioning.

Instead they waited until three in the morning and then came hammering on the gate of the Hotel Manila in Chittagong. I was woken by the racket and listened to their voices echoing up the concrete stairwell. There were, as far as I could tell, three of them, and they insisted on looking through the guest book, checking back on the dates and times we'd given them.

Along with the rest of my luggage I'd picked up my address book from the hotel in Cox Bazaar, and, worried about the possible implications for my Bangladeshi friends should the army have decided we were up to no good, I hid it in the passageway outside our room.

I needn't have bothered, the men stayed ten minutes or so and then left without disturbing us.

10

Manipuri

'I am standing here,' the businessman in the corridor of the sluggish train going north announced in English to anyone who would listen, 'because some biting insects have taken very pleased refuge in the cracks in the wooden seating, and they are waiting for fatty people like me to come along. When they see me come they creep out of the cracks and start biting.' He laughed loudly at his plight.

'Let's hope no dacoits creep out of the woodwork in the same fashion.'

'Yes, indeed. Only last week on this train one passenger was killed and many stabbed by dacoits who had been impersonating passengers. Yes, they had been impersonating passengers, and then they suddenly made their presence known.'

He was amusing company until a blind boy who shuffled down the corridor with his hand out was slow to move on when ordered. The man took him by the back of his neck, shook him like a dog, and then thrust him away so forcefully that he fell. The man restrained an impulse to kick him, smiled at me and pointed out that we were passing within two hundred yards of the border with the Indian state of Tripura, the only northeastern state where Bengalis now outnumber tribals. Everyone in the carriage leant forward to look more closely, but there was little enough to see – a few bare hills rising nakedly from the rice fields.

A barefoot, ragged urchin boy pushed past the man, and was cuffed for his lack of respect.

If there's ever a revolution in Bangladesh it will be understandable if those who've been treated with such contempt by the rich go on the rampage and destroy more than they build, or send their tormentors into the countryside to work in the paddy fields, to starve and to slave as they have had to for generations. It makes the things that Pol Pot and his schoolkid cadres did in Cambodia almost understandable (not excusable).

A Manipuri man sitting opposite waited for the businessman to go before speaking. He was, he informed me, starting a new magazine, and could he have my address? I filled in the form a little unwillingly, and when I'd done so, almost as though it were a prize, he drew a picture from the inside pocket of his tattered pin-stripe jacket. He was about thirty, with a thin, skull-like face, and nervously sure of himself – his eyes never rested on anything for more than a moment, and he couldn't keep still. It was tiring just to talk to him. The picture was a poor photocopy of a poor photograph, and meant nothing to me.

'Tangal General,' the Manipuri said.

I must have looked blank, for he continued, 'Tangal General was a Manipuri nationalist hero. He was hung by the British in 1891.'

There was no sense in which this was said to make me uncomfortable. The man smiled – his teeth were crooked and stained with *pan* – and he told the story.

For over thirty years, between 1856 and 1889, Tangal Singh, also known as Tangal General, was the Chief Minister and General of King Kulochando in Manipur. During this period he received many attestations from British officers to his energy, loyalty, faithfulness, efficiency and kindness. A Mrs Grimwood described him as having 'a fine old face, much lined and wrinkled with age ... piercing black eyes, shaggy overhanging white eyebrows, and white hair. His nose was long and slightly hooked, and his mouth was finely cut and very determined.'

The British quite wrongly involved themselves in the Byzantine, fratricidal politics of the royal household, and the political agent (Mrs Grimwood's husband) committed a series of errors which culminated in the Tangal General putting him and four others to death. Although Manipur was an independent state, this became known in Britain as the 1891 Manipur Mutiny. A short campaign ensued, and the eighty-six-year-old Tangal lost, of course, to the superior arms of the British. A canon – dragged up from the plains – did particular damage. He was tried, and along with one of the Manipur princes, convicted and sentenced to death for waging war against the Queen Empress of India, and for the murder of British officers.

I looked up the case when I returned to London, and found that even at the time the trial had caused a storm of criticism, mostly because Britain had no legal jurisdiction in Manipur, and because the Tangal was denied a counsel for the defence. One (English) contemporary commented that it was 'One of the most outrageous farces and parodies of justice that have yet been exhibited to the Indian nation'.

Which was saying something.

A moving and callous account of Tangal's hanging was left by Lieutenant Colonel Alban Wilson DCO in his memoirs, *Sports and Service in Assam
and Elsewhere*:

A guard of four hundred rifles surrounded the scaffold, as it was expected there
might be an attempt at rescue. The Tangal pretended to be too ill to walk up
to the gallows, and was carried up in a chair and placed beneath the noose ...
A sergeant of gunners, who was executioner, tapped the Tangal General on
the shoulder and said, 'Now then, old man, stand up or I can't hang you.'
The Tangal gazed at him blankly, and then at the interpreter who translated
the remark, on which the old fellow shook his head and roared with laughter.
The interpreter said, 'Sir, the General states he will not rise.'
The sergeant said, most persuasively, 'Just tell the old gentleman I'm not
going to hurt him.' This too, was translated, but the Tangal would not budge.
Then ensued the most ghastly pause, whilst a man climbed up to the top of
the gallows to lengthen the rope, and when it was adjusted both criminals were
loosed off.

Wilson writes that the Manipuri were pleased to see the back of the
Tangal, whom he describes as cruel in the extreme, but the examples he
gives seem standard for the time, whether perpetrated by British, Manipuri
or anyone else.

It was a long rickshaw ride over sandy tracks from the rural station where
we alighted to the Manipuri village. The path zigzagged past an ornate
mosque inlaid with broken porcelain, and past an abandoned Hindu
temple being used as a cow byre by a Muslim family; the niches where
the gods had once stood were dustily empty, hay rakes stood propped in
a corner, and the straw squelched underfoot. Further on the houses
changed from the usual mud structures to half-timbered, substantial affairs
infilled with bamboo and plaster, and painted white. Beside them were
bamboo poles from which hung long flags made of split bamboo and
white netting, like Tibetan prayer flags – operating as some kind of spirit
filter. Paper flowers decorated their bottom edges. The vegetable gardens
were immaculately kept, and superficially the households looked rich: the
buildings were large, and there was cut rice stored on racks in the clean,
swept yards.
Two Manipuri women weaving on back-strap looms outside their house
smiled vaguely at us but continued to work. We were carrying letters of
introduction to three individuals, and the older of the two women sent a
child to find out if they were around, at the same time ordering another

to fetch two chairs for us. They were most insistent that we should sit on the chairs in the shade of their veranda rather than wander about in the sun, so we sat. Talk didn't seem to matter to them much; they asked a few questions, but they were slow, village people used to taking their time. There was no reason for things to happen quickly in their world.

A daughter fed us oranges and tea, and showed us examples of the women's weaving: striped skirts with black and red woven borders of such detail that they looked embroidered. The cloth itself was soft, but the weave so tight as to be almost invisible. Then she took us for a walk around the village, which consisted of two wide, parallel paths overhung by bamboos and trees. Every house had a flower garden, roses, bougainvillaea, hibiscus and *tulsi* – the plant of Hindu devotion – and the appearance of wealth may have been created by this element of decoration. A flower garden is rare to all but a rich Bengali Muslim house. Although the Manipuri women were all well turned out in reds and pinks and blues, the men gave the game away – if they weren't dressed traditionally in a short lungi and a heavy cotton shawl then they wore ragged, second-hand Western clothes.

By the time we returned to our bags one of our contacts had turned up. Her name was Santana, and she and her sister were doctors at the local health centre. They were both full of life and attractive in different ways; Santana had the perfect complexion, long features and almond-shaped eyes of the Manipuri, while the other, Kanju, was darker and more Aryan looking, although she too had high cheekbones and fine eyes. They said that they weren't married because they were too ugly, and only later did one get serious enough to admit that they were happy as they were – life was much harder for married women, they said.

The women's uncle, Lairik-yem-bum (the man who looks at books), was in charge, and he got down to the nitty-gritty straight away. He was keen to know exactly what we were up to, convinced that anyone writing a book must be an academic, that I must have an hypothesis to test. What kind of questionnaires would have to be filled in? he asked. And how much did I know already? He wanted me to ask him questions, but I didn't have any, and it took him time to understand the idea of simply being there, of looking around and talking to Manipuri about their lives.

It was almost dark, and we sat beside the courtyard of the family's house watching a theatrical scene. The backdrop was the veranda on which stood a small table, a hookah and a chair, as though awaiting the entrance of the leading actor. The set was lit by two hurricane lamps which cast a weird greenish glow over the figures and animals. On the floor of the veranda sat Lairik's wizened father, with thick, pebbled glasses, and much grey stubble. In one hand he held a heavy stick, which he used to emphasize his orders.

Behind the house, above the corrugated iron roof, bamboos curled over in mimicry of sea shells, and front of stage three buffalo, roped side by side, circled solemnly, held tightly in check and forced round by a young man, a son-in-law, wielding a whip. A servant untied stooks of rice and piled the loose ears beneath the feet of the animals, to husk the grain.

The old man shouted irritably at them all, 'Pay attention!', 'Not that way!', 'Use your brain!', and thumped the hollow wooden veranda with his stick. It was like the beginning of an Ibsen play, as though tragedy and repressed passion, hatred or love, lurked in the characters' lives, in their usage of each other, and was about to burst into violence.

Lairik, Santana and Kanju were educated people, and had a clearer idea of who and what they were than any of the other minorities we'd met so far. Our arrival was important to them – it was a chance to explain themselves to outsiders, however insignificant, and they treated us seriously – in fact so seriously that it was some time before I realized that their questions weren't prompted by suspicion of our motives, but by a desire to be as helpful as possible. Even so no one had said anything about being able to stay in the village, and it was getting late, so I had to ask straight out.

They were shocked, 'Of course, that's arranged, there's no doubt about it,' Santana replied, apologizing at the same time for the quality of the accommodation. 'The bed is hard, and the room small, so how can you sleep? Also, there's no sofa set, or television, or even electricity. I'm sure it will be a problem for you.'

We reassured her, but there was more. 'And then how can we entertain you? We're only village girls.'

'What does that mean?' I asked.

She came back fast, 'It means we can plant and cut rice, weed, grow vegetables, weave, cook, sing and work in the hospital. The only thing I can't do is drive a car, but when I go to London I'll learn that too, then I'll be fulfilled.'

She had no real desire to go to London, although she would have liked the opportunity to drive a car.

'Your arrival is like a dream for us,' Kanju added sweetly, and I assured her that it was like a dream for me too, that it had taken more than a year to organize the trip.

In the following few days Lairik introduced us around the village, and

123

one day he took us to see an old man, a carpenter. The man sat cross-legged on an ancient, multi-coloured woollen mat near his house, surrounded by all he required. On one side, in a hole in the ground, was a fire, and balanced on the hole a kettle containing tea. On his other side a brass box held betel leaves, areca nuts, lime and nut clippers. In a wooden box at his feet were a variety of high-quality, imported tools, Stanley planes and the like, while his wood store was behind him. Lairik was proud of the carpenter, but also a little embarrassed by his eccentricity, unsure how we'd react.

The old man's abundant grey hair was covered by a thick woolly hat of some indeterminate colour, once purple perhaps, and he had the dramatic energy of a wrestler, combined with the grace of someone who works with all their limbs – a piece of wood was held fast in the vice of his feet all the time we were there. He spoke loudly, and sometimes slipped from Bengali into Hindi, excusing himself, when reminded by Lairik, on the grounds that the tea garden sahibs had always spoken Hindi – he'd learnt his trade as a young man in the gardens.

The carpenter was an autodidact, and he exuded a sense of well-being and contentment. The most important place in the world, as far as he was concerned, was where he was. He wasn't on any desperate search for some unattainable end, and seemed to have most of what he wanted; his life, his religion, his beliefs and his philosophy were centred. He desired nothing more, neither possessions nor money. No great conflicts pulled him one way or the other; he knew what it was to be a Manipuri, and where he stood in the world. At least so he seemed to me.

'The other word for Manipuri is Meithei,' he explained, 'and that means a man detached from the image of god, or a man distinct from other people.' This was how he, and other Manipuri seemed to see themselves – detached, separate, distinct from all other types and kinds of human beings. They were clearly defined, independent individuals, in a way which few people in tight clan or family groups are able to be, and this was most noticeable with the women, who weren't watched and guarded from thieves and their own supposed stupidity like cows or sheep, as Muslim women are.

The carpenter was a devotee of the Manipuri religion, Apokpa, and he collected books and materials on the subject, which he produced for our inspection. They included some finely drawn pen and ink designs which he'd done himself: one showed a bull eating its own tail in a meditative sort of way. When I said I thought that most Manipuri were Hindu he denied it hotly, conceding only that some might be Vaishnavites – devotees

124

of Vishnu, who emphasize the dignity and equality of all people, in stark contrast to other forms of Hinduism. 'But they're also followers of Apokpa,' he added, drawing a plan of a Manipuri house in the dust with a stick. 'Here,' he said, jabbing the earth, 'in every house will be the household god, the sun god, Sanamahi. And here, outside every house,' the stick marked the dust again, 'is the shrine of the moon god, Pakhamba.'

When I made the mistake of referring to the Manipuri as tribal people, I was gently corrected.

'We aren't tribals, we are a nation. We have our own culture, history and traditions. We have never practised *jhum* agriculture, and we're not like others, we're not like the Mizo, Naga, Mandi, Chakma or the Mru.'

All the Manipuri we met were insistent on this point, but anthropologists are in little doubt that the Manipuri are closely related to the Naga, in the neighbouring state.

In Bangladesh the Manipuri had another identity problem.

'The government says it will give us special help if we accept the definition tribal. We won't, but there's a group of people called Bishnupriya, who say they are Manipuri, and who do accept the tribal tag. So they've been adopted by the government as their pet Manipuri. But they speak an Indo-Aryan language, where Manipuri has a Tibeto-Burmese root. Not only that, if there's a cultural event in Dhaka then the Bishnupriya are wheeled out to perform some so-called Manipuri dances. They don't know any Manipuri dances though – they dance Bengali dances – so now all Bengalis think that Manipuri culture is just an inferior version of Bengali culture. It confirms them in their prejudices.'

When I reached the Madhupur Forest a month later I discovered that the same trick, or something similar was being played on the Mandi people.

The Manipuri in Bangladesh arrived in Sylhet in 1824. They were refugees, and had fled Imphal after losing a battle between brothers for the succession to the throne. Someone told me that the original refugees had consisted of members of the royal court and their servants – who would have been of different castes. Perhaps the Bishnupriya were the descendents of those servants.

Lairik tried to show us everything, from how their houses were constructed, to the medicinal uses of plants he grew in his garden, to recipes (banana flower curry – yum!), to stories and proverbs.

'We have a proverb which goes, "Don't spit in the sky, or you'll get it in the eye", and it fits us well, because we Manipuri in Bangladesh are very isolated. Our forefathers ran away from Imphal, the capital of

Manipur, and now when we go there we're looked down on. The Manipuri in Manipur think of us as Bengalis because we've picked up the practice of speaking loudly like Bengalis. True Manipuri speak softly and melodically.'

One day I came across Lairik's eight-year-old son and a number of naughty-looking friends sitting in a row near the house. Beside them were dozens of mud balls, the size of walnuts. They were waiting patiently for the sun to dry the balls hard, so that they could be used as catapult ammo. They were dead shots, and I persuaded one to loose off a salvo at Peter when he wasn't looking, but Lairik saw him, and I had to intervene to prevent severe punishment being meted out. Lairik wouldn't or couldn't believe that it was my fault; it didn't fit in with his concept of adult dignity, and he was convinced to the last that I was simply protecting the boy.

The isolation that Lairik described became clearer later when Santana and Kanju sang for us one evening, accompanying themselves on a harmonium; they didn't know any Manipuri songs, only translations into Manipuri of traditional Bengali songs.

'Only now,' Lairik said, 'are people in this village starting to try and learn about our own culture and religion. But we're isolated in two ways, first because we have to cross Assam before we reach Manipur – it's not just across the border so we can't easily get books or information about our own history – and second because this wasn't our original country, unlike most of the other minorities. But now,' he conceded, 'we are Bangladeshis, we have no choice.'

It was a low misty day, the trees on the horizon were barely visible. In the all enveloping greyness, and on the flat land, the buffaloes took on a primeval quality, looking like herds of bison. Apart from the reds and pinks of the women's clothes there were no bright colours as we walked across the fields of cut rice, acres of flat gold interspersed with bamboo stands which marked out the villages. In most places the farmers had harvested only the ears, leaving the stalks, and much grain had fallen, had been left lying among the straw. I remembered my amazement when I first saw people gleaning rice from a field in Bangladesh, and realized that there was an English word for this back-breaking and unrewarding job; that the same level of rural poverty, of desperation had existed in Britain little more than a generation ago.

Lairik had announced that we would go to see the first Manipuri to graduate, in 1939, from Calcutta University. 'He's a Manipuri Muslim.

There aren't many of them, but they're the descendants of Manipuri women and Persian mercenary soldiers who'd been employed by our king two or three centuries ago.'

The man had a splendidly lined face, and the lines converged around the corners of his eyes, as though he was smiling all the time. Otherwise he looked like a bandit: he had a thick white beard, a piece of red cloth wound round his head and a dark blue shawl over his shoulders. He had a hooked nose, and looked as unlike the other Manipuris we'd met as was possible – the central Asian genes were still working strongly in him and his family.

He was silent for a long time when asked to tell me about his life, and I thought he hadn't heard – he was a little deaf – but he interrupted when I started to repeat the question. He spoke in English although he'd had no opportunity to practise it for twenty years.

'There is nothing to say. When I look back on my life I see that I have done nothing, either good or bad. That is why I am silent. When I grew old I thought that perhaps mysticism was the answer. My father believed in the power of mysticism, but I find that it is not the answer either.'

We sat on the veranda, and beyond the old man, past the carved wooden door, in the gloomy interior of the house, a teenage boy sat on a chair drooling, smiling and laughing to himself – perhaps inbreeding had caused his disability; there aren't that many Manipuri Muslims in the world, and even fewer in Bangladesh. Outside, in the courtyard, three men were winnowing a great mound of rice; one poured grain onto the pile, while the others fanned the chaff away with violent sweeps of their woven, bamboo trays. Meanwhile the old man's granddaughters, as graceful and startling as young animals, brought tea and puffed rice, a plate for each of us. They looked Persian rather than south or southeast Asian.

The man stared into the courtyard. 'I have not been a man of action in my life. My father would not let me do physical work, or learn any-thing about farming. Once, as a child, I went to give the ploughman some tobacco, and while he was filling his hookah I held the handle of his plough. My father saw me and shouted angrily, "Here! You! What are you doing? Come inside and study." He thought that if I did any physical work it would distract me from my books.'

After I'd tried asking the old man a few questions it became obvious that there was no need – he would tell me what he wanted to tell me, and nothing else. As the oldest person present, and therefore the teacher, his role was to impart knowledge and wisdom; mine was to listen and learn.

'Mohammed, blessed be his name, said that a man riding on a camel, or on an elephant, or by extension in a car, should salute a man on foot first. The Prophet knew that a man who is riding is already proud of his wealth and position, so if the man on foot saluted him first then he would think, "Now I am a nawab", and he would be even more puffed up – such pride is hateful to Allah.

'Once I was walking on the path near my house, and a *maulvi*, a religious teacher, approached on a horse. I thought to myself, "Ah, he must salute me first", and he obviously thought the same, so we passed without a salaam.'

He laughed strongly, showing three teeth spaced evenly through his mouth, and Lairik laughed so much he nearly choked on the puffed rice.

'When I got my degree I tried to find a job in Calcutta, but I did not know about bribes, and I could not find a job until someone explained that I should pay a bribe. "Is it?" I asked in amazement, and the man laughed and he gave me a job.

'The world is a garden, and mankind is like some of the flowers in the garden – some are red, some blue, some yellow, all colours, but actually they are all flowers. The differences between men are exaggerated. The only things which matter are character and behaviour. Look at us, Lairik is a Hindu, I am a Muslim, you are a Christian – but there is no real difference between any of us.'

He'd talked a lot, and was beginning to tire. The light had faded too, and it was time for us to leave. He clasped my hands for a moment, like an old friend, and we left him staring out over the mound of rice in his courtyard. In the high, central room behind him his grandson drooled and swayed on his chair, moved by storms only he could feel.

We'd forgotten to take a torch, and twice the water in the canal running beside the path rippled the stars as a snake slithered from beneath our feet.

We'd agreed to leave early in the morning but Lairik caught some fish from the pond behind his house, and then insisted that we stay to lunch to eat them. Having started out as a nervous host he'd got used to our ways, and was going to miss us – we'd brought news, stories and information from the outside world, and he envied us our lives. After we'd eaten, we sat on his veranda chewing *pan* until there were no more excuses to stay and we had to leave, to walk across a couple of tea gardens to the nearest road.

We'd been cocooned in the shady lanes of the village and by Lairik's hospitality for three days, and the tea garden was a different world. It went on for miles and miles: rolling hills, lines of tea bushes, all trimmed to the same height and shape, looking from a distance like an English lawn, and the feathery, acacia shade trees. Tea garden workers, dark skinned Koira women with gold rings in their noses, acknowledged our presence with little more than a sideways flick of their eyes as they passed. We walked until we came to the road, made up in patches, but in reality little more than a track which wound through the forest. There we hitched a lift on a passing jeep to the nearest town, where a train would take us north, nearer to the Khasi Hills.

11

Tamabil and Beyond

There were no hotels on the northern border, and I had no good contacts, so I had to get permission from the District Council Chairman, the most powerful official in the district, to stay in the government rest house at Tamabil. His large, air-conditioned office, when I found it, was full of schoolgirls. They were trying to persuade him to pay for their class to go on a freebie (they called it a study tour) to Cox Bazaar.

On the wall behind the Chairman hung the regulation photograph of President Ershad looking statesmanlike in a blue jacket; the Chairman, a political appointee, had the same look. He refused the girls politely, arguing that there wasn't enough money in the budget, and although they fought back bravely he wasn't to be moved.

Once they'd left the Chairman turned to me, and the entire administration of the district came to a grinding halt while we chatted about the European cities he'd been to: London, Paris and Dublin. After an hour he released me into the care of his Secretary, a man with a lock of Yeats-like grey hair flopping over his forehead, and ordered him to write out the necessary permission. I waited in the Secretary's office while he bashed away on an ancient Remington typewriter, and several other, unidentified men joined us there; one borrowed his friend's dark glasses to wear while he talked to me. He wanted to know whether I'd have a guide for the area – he regarded Tamabil as a wild and savage place – but he wasn't interested in my reply and kept lapsing into memories of Southsea, where he'd once spent six months on a course. Mostly he remembered how cold it had been.

Once the permission had been typed in triplicate, signed and stamped two or three times the Secretary gave me a copy. 'We will send a runner to Tamabil to inform the guard of your imminent arrival,' he said. 'Please enjoy your stay.' This sentiment was echoed by the man in dark glasses and his friends, who accompanied me from the Secretary's office to the top of the stairs, shook my hand and wished me a pleasant journey. Sometimes things go easily in Bangladesh, and sometimes they don't. There isn't any way of predicting.

On our way to Tamabil we stopped at a village where an American, Catholic priest lived. I'd been given his name by a friend, who said that if he couldn't introduce me to some Khasi then no one could. The priest was called George, and he greeted me like an old friend; perhaps he thought we'd met before, as so many aid workers and embassy officials, did pass through the mission. He'd been in the country since 1936, seeing it go through several incarnations: from East Bengal to East Pakistan, and now Bangladesh. On the walls of the dining room hung a photograph of the Pope, and a picture of Mary Magdalene; the artist had got carried away with her beauty and the halo was hardly visible. There was also a gory picture of Jesus's bleeding heart – the kind of thing you'd expect to see in a farmhouse in Ireland – and other photographs of mountains and glaciers.

Father George wasn't an intellectual or a combative person; he saw his mission in terms of conversion work among the Khasi, not in terms of human rights or any other issue, unlike the priest I met when I reached the Madhupur Forest. His emotional strength came from being north American, and although his mission was for God, it was also for God-and-the-north-American way of life, or so it seemed to me.

The priest's knowledge of the country he lived in was limited to the aspects which would help him in his work, and that didn't include being able to read or write Bengali – although he could speak it fluently. He'd spent the greater part of his life in Bengal, but the literature, the songs and poetry, the culture of which Bengalis are justly proud, had passed him by.

He did take us to a Khasi village though. His driver brought an ancient grey Landrover round to the front of the mission, and drove us out of the village, and into a tea garden, pulling up at a path leading into the forest, a mixture of hardwood and areca nut trees, with broad, heart-leaved creepers trained up them. We got out to walk. The creepers were betel, the leaves of which are used to wrap areca nut and other substances before being chewed as *pan*. Father George explained that plantations of this kind are known by the Khasi as *punji*. The wettest place in the world is a Khasi town, Cherrapunji, across the border in Meghalaya, India; *cherra* means stream or water, so the name translates as 'the plantation by the stream'. The village he was taking us to was called Seguncherra punji, or 'the plantation by the stream in the teak (*segun*) forest'.

Pan is chewed all over the subcontinent, and the areca nut and betel leaf business is a profitable one, although it doesn't make the Khasi particularly rich.

Father George explained that the attitude of the local Bengali population to the Khasi was complicated. 'Of course they often try to cheat the Khasi in the way of business, but generally only middle-class Bengalis see them as untutored savages. The rest, I mean ordinary Bengali peasants, respect the Khasi because they see that their way of life is superior to their own – that the Khasi live better. The Khasi are great individualists, and don't like being beholden to anyone, especially not to Bengalis. No Khasi will work for a Bengali, they'd rather starve, and they don't usually employ Bengalis to collect the areca or betel.

'The Khasi themselves are like monkeys in the trees; they're brought up to clamber about up there, but if they do need to employ help then they get Mandi people to work for them, and the Mandi are less adept so they often fall, killing or maiming themselves.'

The Mandi (or Garo) tribal people inhabit the western hills of Meghalaya, India, but like the Khasi they've traditionally occupied large areas of forest further south, in the plains. Father George said that there was little sympathy between the two tribal groups, and he gave as an example the rejection of children born to Khasi mothers by Mandi fathers, or vice versa. He described how one boy in Seguncherra punji had been given to him as a baby by the dying mother. The mother was a Mandi, but as the father was a Khasi she knew that neither side would accept the baby. The child had ended up in America. He was now eighteen, and he wrote to his father sometimes. In the village the boy's father proudly showed us photographs of his strapping son, in the football team, by the pool with his blonde American sisters, and playing the fool with his friends.

The path wound through the forest of tall trees, with a light, almost silver bark; green shadows and yellow sunlight splashed the sandy ground, and the honey smell of some jungle flower wafted past on a slight breeze. It was quiet, even the birds were resting, and the sight of the village came as a surprise.

A steep flight of log-supported steps led to the top of a small hill. We climbed slowly and entered a village of wood and mud houses, where Father George underwent a change: he became the picture of a noisy, jolly Catholic priest at work, and the people we met were deferential to him.

'Only about half the village is Christian,' he said sadly. 'The rest are pagans. My work goes very slowly. But anyway look at their traditional clothing.'

What did he see? With the exception of one or two women who wore a kind of knee-length shawl tied over one shoulder, in the same style as the Mru women, no one was wearing traditional clothes. The men were in trousers and shirts, and the women wore knee-length dresses – the kind of thing you'd have seen at a village fete in the Home Counties thirty years ago, second-hand Western clothes imported either through the medium of the Church, or commercially.

I found it creepy to be greeted by everyone, whether Christian or animist, with a word which the Father insisted meant 'God Bless You', denying that the Khasi had any other greeting. Among the Mandi in the Madhupur Forest a month later I found the same thing; that an overtly Christian greeting had become the norm for everyone, to the extent that they'd lost one of the most basic words in their own language – which did, of course, exist.

A kind of lethargy permeated the village; there was a hopelessness about the place, as though it was sinking into despair, or dying in some way, and I felt that Father George was compensating for this by putting on his happy, jolly act. The impression I got was of a deracinated people, of a people in the process of swopping their traditions for the obvious power of the West, symbolized by religion and clothing. The West offers material benefits, and they were able to tap Western sources of money and power more effectively through the Church than through their host society.

We left Father George, hoping that not all Khasi villages were going to be as depressing as this one.

The Tamabil Zilla Parishad Rest House, to give it its full title, turned out to be an ugly concrete building – a feat of engineering rather than of architecture or design – set on a magnificent site at the top of an isolated hill. Half a mile away were the Khasi Hills in India, rising steeply out of the plain, covered in jungle, and *punji*. Two miles beyond the Rest House was the border crossing point, where small children played football on both sides, and rolled their hoops under and around the road barrier, marked in Bengali and English 'Vehicles Only'. Down the broad river valley, dotted through the fields, were concrete border markers, painted white, like large mushrooms.

I was surprised to find a woman running a tea shop by the side of the road in Tamabil, where the bus dropped us – I'd never seen it anywhere else in Bangladesh. She was strikingly good looking, and had an odd, challenging manner. Her father had been a Punjabi soldier based at the border, she told us, but he'd been killed during the 1971 Liberation War, while her mother had been a Bihari. She was therefore doubly damned, first for being Punjabi, the oppressors of the pre-Bangladesh days, and second for being Bihari, who had sided with the Pakistanis. She'd been six when her father was killed, and had been through much in her twenty-five years. Her husband was half Khasi, half Bengali, but she complained to us that he was crazy, and it was true that he didn't seem to be all there. 'But I'm mad too,' she said, raising her chin. 'Don't you think I'm mad?'

It was her defence mechanism, and had perhaps got her out of difficult situations in the past. She was allowed some leeway because she acted as though she was mad – at least in the eyes of the tough men around her, the border police, the smugglers and get-rich-quick merchants who frequented her tea shop and store. Any woman who behaved as provocatively and defiantly as she did, merely by running a tea shop, had to be mad. I liked her. She was a person in her own right, and didn't seem to be that bothered by what people thought of her, although perhaps that came about through force of circumstance rather than choice. The difference between her and the *hijra* was that whereas the latter have an accepted, structured role in society, this woman had had to create her own structure, build her own rules and barriers against a society which would have otherwise crushed her. It was sad, because in reality she was surviving in the only way possible, apart from prostitution.

'Take me to England with you,' she demanded.

'What about your children?'

'I'll go for ten years, then come back. My husband can look after them. Or maybe I'll take the baby, just the baby. Will you take me?'

'It's too cold. You wouldn't like it.'

'I would. I don't mind the cold.'

'What would you do there?'

'Cook, run a tea shop. The same as here. It's no good here.'

'But you're doing OK. Look, you have a house, you have goods to sell, a secure life.'

She laughed. 'Yes, three weeks ago thieves came in the night and stole everything. They took the complete stock, three thousand *taka* worth. Very secure.'

Over the next few days I saw how hard the reality was; to the police and the border guards she was fair game – no one admired her courage, or wanted to help her. In fact the opposite was true for she threatened the established order by proving that an ordinary, uneducated woman could survive in the open.

'She's a very bad woman,' the Rest House guard said, and this was echoed by several local men who came to sit and talk to us on the veranda in the evenings. We were never sure who they were, these men who appeared out of the night – there was no electricity and only one hurricane lamp so we didn't see their faces clearly.

One arranged to get us a bottle of Chinese gin from across the border, and he explained how the system worked. 'You give your order now,' he said, 'and tomorrow morning a child will cross the border with a chicken – chickens are worth fifty *taka* on this side and seventy on the other – and will come back with your bottle. It's simple. No one bothers with the children.'

He agreed with the guard that the woman was a bad character, adding as evidence that she was mixed up with the customs officials and smugglers (the two were interchangeable as far as he was concerned). He didn't regard himself as a bad character despite his own smuggling activities on our behalf.

The men liked to talk politics with us; they hated President Ershad and his government, but were under no illusions about the opposition, or opposition politicians. 'We go on strike, we fight, we get killed in demonstrations,' said one, 'and these famous politicians, lawyers and businessmen who claim to represent us, who call themselves our leaders, send their children abroad to be educated. They don't take any risks with their lives, with their money or their politics.' And he spat into the night.

When I asked about the Khasi the men were unanimous in their praise, and the guard summed it up by saying, 'They're very good, honest people, not like us Bengalis.' The others nodded in agreement. 'They think about the future. A Khasi will never cut down a tree, but a Bengali farmer will cut down a tree because he can sell the wood for three thousand *taka*, forgetting the fruit which he could have sold for twenty years.'

Someone interrupted, 'Khasi women do most of the work, they're also very beautiful.'

'So why aren't you all married to Khasi women?' I asked.

The men laughed. 'They're not so easy to get! They don't like us much, and then they have to change their religion if they marry a Muslim. There is one Muslim married to a Khasi in a village a few miles away. His wife does everything; the areca nut business, the cooking, cleaning, marketing, everything.'

'So what does he do?'

'Him? He doesn't do anything. He rests all day, and then in the evening he sleeps. If he wants a new shirt, or to go to the cinema he asks his wife for the money, and she gives it to him. What a life!'

Another continued on the same theme. 'The Khasi are rich, but they don't show it off like we Muslims do. At our Eid festival, for example, rich Muslims compete to spend the greatest amount of money on a cow or a bullock. But what's the point? It's just to impress their friends, it's got nothing to do with Islam. And who profits? The Hindus who smuggle the cows in from India!'

They all laughed at that, and after a few more dry comments they drifted off into the night, which reverberated with the sound of a thousand crickets, the eerie howl of a jackal, and from somewhere deep within a *punji*, an insistent, throbbing drum beat.

The guard told us that the drumming came from a Khasi village across the border. Did we want to go there?

We did, but wouldn't we have a problem with the border police who were supposed to patrol the area? He snorted, and waved his hand like a conjurer disappearing a couple of doves, 'They don't go out after dark.'

Wondering whether this information was in the same category as, 'The army does't work on Sundays', but deciding we could claim ignorance, we walked down the hill with him.

It was a couple of miles, and it was odd to walk towards the Khasi Hills, rising like a black wall in front of us, as though they might suddenly open, split wide, revealing an underground kingdom. The drumming stopped long before we reached the village, but in a small house the drinking was still going on. Peter quickly fell in with a rowdy group of Khasi who spoke Nepali – one of his languages – and they got on famously. They'd learnt Nepali, they said, by working on road gangs with Nepalese down from their Himalayan villages for the same reason. It was hard work, but it paid relatively well, and they'd all come home with cash in their pockets. Now they were drinking it away.

A tall Khasi introduced himself as Steven. He had a financial interest in the stone business which was the main economic stay of the Bangladesh side.

'Stone's valuable because it's in such short supply,' he explained. 'There just isn't any rock, except in the Dawki River at Bhorlaghat.' Steven spoke English with an Italian accent, rolling his Rs and pronouncing each letter. He'd been taught the language at school in Shillong by an Italian missionary. He soon got bored of talking about his business, and started to assassinate the Bengali character to his friend, a Bengali. 'They are all cheaters,' he insisted. 'There are three kinds of cheater: first there are the labourers, then there are the suppliers of stones, and then there are the contractors and truck owners.'

The Bengali laughed cheerfully and nodded his head in vigorous agreement. 'Yes, yes, we are most zigzag [actually he said jig-jag] people.'

Steven wasn't to be put off his stride by this interruption. 'Only I have a clever enough mind to be sure they don't cheat me. Still they try. They are most bad people. Nowhere else in the world are there such bad people.'

'Do you agree with that?' I asked the Bengali.

He nodded. 'Yes, I am a Bengali, but I cannot say that it isn't true.'

Steven was incensed that I should doubt his word, 'Of course it's true! I am not telling lies. Khasi people do not lie. We are straight people, we do what we say. That's why it's easy to cheat us. If a Bengali says he will do something for you and later you ask why he didn't do it, he'll say "Oh, I only said that because I was in trouble and needed your help. Now I'm out of trouble so why should I help you?"'

Throughout this tirade the Bengali was nodding and chewing *pan* alternately. 'And they will never help each other. If one Bengali is in trouble all the others will be seeing how they can get his land cheaply, or his house, or his wife.'

I glanced at the Bengali, but he was still nodding and smiling, showing his teeth, stained red with *pan*.

'If you go to a hundred Khasi houses you won't see any difference. You'll never be able to tell who's rich and who's poor because we help each other.'

'But you are a Bangladeshi,' I reminded Steven.

'I'm a Khasi,' he said stubbornly.

'And actually I'm a Hindu,' the Bengali said in the rather uncomfortable silence which followed. 'But I'm still a Bangladeshi, and so are you.'

Steven was adamant. 'I am a Khasi, a tribal.'

'We Hindus are facing many problems because we are a minority across the border. Muslims steal our land, our crops, anything they can.'

Steven wasn't interested in the problems of others, and he spoke as though you had to be stupid to allow yourself to be mistreated. 'We Khasi have no dealings with Bengalis if we can help it. Only I do because I am more clever than they are. OK, so we sell betel leaves and areca nuts and oranges in the market, but we tell a price and that's it. No bargaining. What for is bargaining?'

In another corner of the drinking den, near Peter, a Khasi and a Bengali man were squaring up to each other; they were both as drunk as it's possible to be without falling over, and we left in case it got serious and the police turned up.

The next morning we decided to go to Bhorlaghat to see the stonefields. Three Khasi women got onto the bus with us, with much laughter and chatter. They were weighed down with bags of oranges, areca nuts and betel leaves. The men on the bus, Bengalis, teased them, stole oranges from their bags, and asked for free *pan*. It was all done with good humour, and they got their *pan*, and tried to take more – *pan* was practically free in the area there was so much of it. At the restaurants in Bhorlaghat it was given away to people who ate, and I developed a taste for it.

In the cities of Bangladesh and northern India *pan* is eaten with all kinds of additions: tobacco, chemical sweeteners, rose-water, gold and silver leaf, catechu, cardamom, and camphor, to name but a few. Eaten fresh, without additions, it's a very different thing. But the additions are necessary in the cities because if the nuts are not fresh they become hard and unpleasant and the leaves tasteless.

The areca nut, about the same size as a nutmeg, is chopped into quarters or smaller with a special pair of clippers, wrapped in a betel leaf and eaten, with or without the addition of quicklime. It's an innocuous narcotic which gives a slight, instant buzz, but it wears off quickly. Among the poor it's used to ward off the pangs of hunger, but it's taken by all classes. Even Marco Polo reported that all the people 'Have a custom of perpetually keeping in the mouth a certain leaf . . . the lords and gentlefolks and the King have these leaves prepared with camphor and other aromatic spices, and also mixt with quicklime . . .'

Bhorlaghat consisted of a Bangladesh Border Rifles' post, four or five tea shops and restaurants, and some stone traders' offices. The Dawki River marks the border between Bangladesh and India, but the hundreds of trucks and boats and black figures working like ants dominated the scene, packed onto a right-angled bend in the river, where it sweeps towards the Khasi Hills and is rebuffed, forced to turn south.

This isolated northeastern corner is Bangladesh's equivalent of the Klondyke. We couldn't find Steven, but another Khasi, called Ari, latched onto us.

'Every day,' he explained, 'the trucks are loaded up by labourers working for people who lease a strip of river bank.'

The labourers included workers from the tea estates nearby: narrow-waisted, erect young women in tattered saris, reminiscent of the frescos of idealized women in the Buddhist caves at Ajanta in India. For the most part the tea garden workers aren't Muslims, they're Orya, and Koira –

brought from the Indian states of Orissa and Uttar Pradesh three or four generations ago by the British.

Three women were working below where Ari and I stood on the river bank – Peter had disappeared into the chaos of trucks, boats, boulders and water.

One of the women took a boulder out of the narrow boat moored to the bank, lifted it onto the cloth wound around her head and walked up a steep path. At the top she passed it to another woman who took it fifty yards to where a third carried it to a truck. They didn't work fast, but at a pace they could sustain all day. Other women and men worked on the margins of the river itself, shovelling gravel, or humping boulders into the boats and trucks moored and parked beside each other. Stone dust hung over the entire scene, watering down the colour of a cool-looking areca nut plantation on the far shore. The *punji* looked like a mirage; it shimmered over the desolation and destruction, over a desert of stone and dust, through which the river ran like an irrelevance – it had been so dug up, diverted, and dammed that it had no form, no identity, except that given by its dangerous, icy blue.

'Come,' Ari said, 'come to my village.'

We walked through the *punji* beside the river. On the water itself a pale fire blazed at one end of a boat, and a man dived off it deep into the centre of the Dawki. A minute later he reappeared with a boulder, and as soon as it had been taken off him by another man in the boat he sank below the water again. It was like a gross caricature of diving for pearls. After four or five boulders had been brought up he had to get out and stand beside the fire to warm up. He was a well-built man, but a few minutes in the freezing water had shrivelled his muscles. His broad, black back curved inwards and he shivered uncontrollably, like someone in shock. Ten minutes later the fire and the sun had made little difference, but down he had to go again – in the necessary pursuit of his own death.

I asked Ari whether he was involved in the stone business.

'No Khasi will do this work,' came the rather taciturn response.

He didn't want to continue the discussion, but I asked whether it was because Khasi people wouldn't work for Bengali businessmen.

He gestured at the dust-laden air, at the noisy trucks, at the wounded river valley, and the milky water. 'It used to be beautiful here. It was quiet and peaceful and the river ran clean.'

'Is that why no Khasi will work here?'

He was silent for a while and then muttered, so that I only just caught it, 'No Khasi will work here because this is Oreng's place.'

139

It sounded like Oreng, but may not have been. I made a wild guess, 'The god of the river?'

'Yes.'

'So the god doesn't like what's happened?'

'He's angry about what's happened to his river. That's why there were floods here last year and the year before. There never used to be floods, but last year three hundred Khasi people drowned – two whole villages were washed away at Bhorlaghat.'

Oreng was not a subject for discussion though; the Khasi's traditional, animist beliefs have been ridiculed over a long period by missionaries, to the extent that they're now unwilling to talk about them at all to outsiders. And what he'd said about the river was true: the stone traders have ripped out the banks of boulders which would have normally provided a defence against flash floods, leaving the villages exposed and vulnerable.

Perhaps Oreng really was angry.

After a twenty-minute walk we reached Ari's village, deep in the heart of a *punji*, a shady and quiet spot, beside the river, where the houses were built on wooden stilts or stone pillars.

Ari marched up to one, where two parrots were chained to a perch hanging below the eaves. They were pretty birds with grey heads and chests, fading to rose, and had a bright red bar on their bills. He hammered on the door, and woke the headman, who turned out to be one of those who'd been squaring up for a fight the previous evening, in the village across the border. He was badly hung over and barely capable of speech, but his mother, a tough old lady, gave me *pan* and complained that all Bengalis were thieves. Ari expanded on this theme, saying that in India, he meant in the Khasi Hills, 'You can leave money lying around and no one will touch it, whereas in Bangladesh a hundred people will jump on it if you leave it for a moment.'

I laughed. It's not my experience of India, where I've lost three passports and any amount of money over the past twelve years.

He took me back to Bhorlaghat through a tea garden, past a vast banyan tree set beside a small pond with red water lotus growing in it, and past tea garden workers' houses, their warm mud walls decorated with ochre hand prints, and circular designs and stripes in white, blue and orange. I tracked Peter down just in time to catch the last truck back to Tamabil. We squatted down on the wet boulders in the back, along with five labourers, and discussed their wages (not enough), the weather in England (cold as the river), and their boss (a crook), before they dropped us by the Punjabi-Bihari woman's tea shop in Tamabil.

She showed us a couple of fish swimming around in a bucket and we asked her to cook them for us. It was midnight before the food was ready, but she managed to retain her energy and good humour, although she'd risen at 6 a.m., worked all day, cooked, looked after three small children, run the shop, and fetched water from across the fields. She again raised the question of coming to England and said she'd cook, clean and do everything for us. She was so serious that I had to explain that we weren't big people with big houses and servants, and this quietened her, although I doubt she believed me.

A man loomed out of the darkness of the road and offered to get us a bottle of Indian rum – we were becoming known – and soon after two Bangladesh Border Rifles' officers came in. They were aggressive to begin with, but quickly calmed down and became quite friendly. I asked them about smuggling.

'There's no smuggling on this road. We import onions, coal and wood, but nothing goes the other way, we export nothing.' He paused, as though reminded of something, 'But the border's long, there's jungle on both sides, and it's not possible to police it all.'

They were less friendly to the woman. One demanded a packet of cigarettes from her, and either because she thought our presence might provide some protection or because she was fed up with their continual demands, maybe both, she reacted badly.

'You had one packet yesterday, and another the day before that,' she said sharply, raising her chin. 'How much do you want to take from me?'

The man was annoyed not to receive the instant obedience and deference he felt was his due, especially in front of two foreigners. He took a packet of cigarettes off a shelf, opened it and offered me one. The woman didn't try to stop him. He then ordered her to give him a box of matches – he could have taken them also, but he wanted to demonstrate his power.

'I don't have any. You've already stolen them all.'

It was a silly piece of defiance, but the only one open to her, and it made the officer even more angry. He went outside and we heard him demand a light from the woman's husband. She shouted through the door, 'The squaddies have taken all the matches, don't give him anything else.'

She must have known that the man and his companion would want to get even for their dented dignity, for being insulted by a woman, and a Punjabi-Bihari at that, but at that moment she didn't care.

When we passed the next day the same men were standing about in the road drinking tea. The woman was in tears, distressed and hysterical, and she talked incoherently about the officers stealing from her. One of them explained that she'd given them five hundred *taka*, and added with a leer, 'for co-operation, you understand?'

12

Tribe to Tribe

We wanted to try and cross northern Bangladesh, by boat or on foot, but knew that we'd have to go further south, away from the sensitive border region, before it would be possible, so we went to Sylhet.

'Hello, you from London then?' asked the young hotelier. He was from Birmingham, over on holiday seeing his father. He wasn't enjoying himself, 'It's so boring, there's nothing to do, and I don't like the way people behave to each other here. They'll try anything on. Know what I mean? When I first got here a couple of months ago they knew I was a foreigner, but I changed pretty quick I can tell you. Changed my clothes, made sure my skin went a bit darker, the lot, otherwise they take advantage. I'm off home in a week, thank God. I can't wait.

'I mean it makes you want to go out and get drunk doesn't it? The place is so screwed down. You can't do what you want to do. Sometimes I feel like acting outrageously just to shake them up a bit. I mean you've got to be able to be a bit of a hooligan sometimes haven't you?' He laughed at the thought. 'But basically I want to get back to my girlfriend. Don't know how you stand it myself. I wouldn't come here if it wasn't for my dad.'

'Hello, I am a singer,' a small man standing at the counter informed me. 'My name is Huda, and I may say that I am very well known, in both Bangladesh and in the UK ...'

I tried to escape, to get to my room, but the singer insisted on telling me about himself. He was probably a good singer, but he wasn't someone who listened, or who was interested in any subject apart from himself. He talked in lists: places he'd been in the UK, songs he'd sung, people he'd met (from Peter Shore MP on), and pubs he'd drunk in. When he'd established his credentials to his own satisfaction he demanded my room number so that he could drop in later on.

I hadn't uttered a word since he'd introduced himself, and I gaped at the hotelier in desperation; he shrugged and said, 'See what I mean?'

It was a cold morning and the mist hung low over the river, deep in its channel. The Bedeh boats were moored against bamboo poles driven into the mud about forty feet offshore, and the two visible adult figures were well wrapped in dark, woollen shawls. I called to one sitting on the prow of the nearest boat. He had a rugged, rough-looking face, but was playing gently with a child aged about two.

I called out, to ask whether we could come over, and the man smiled, 'Yes. Why not? But how are you going to get here?'

He was surprised to see us roll up our trousers and wade out to the boats. Inside one boat a group of five men were playing some form of poker. They weren't Bedeh but had borrowed the boat, they explained, to gamble on, away from the prying eyes of policemen.

'But why do you hide?' I asked. 'Gambling's not forbidden.'

They laughed, and one said, 'You tell the police that! They act as though it were.'

Another added, 'If they're sure you're not powerful it's illegal, but *you* could gamble publicly without any problem.'

'But I'm not powerful.'

He looked at me, and conceded doubtfully that I didn't look like a powerful person. 'Maybe, but you're rich.'

'Not even rich. I'm poor.'

They laughed again. 'If you're poor then what are we? The police would think you were rich, so you'd be all right. Besides you might have good connections. You might know the District Commissioner or someone else important. Then they'd be in trouble for demanding bribes.'

The Bedeh man, Aziz, lived on the boat with his wife, two children and his mother, a spry sixty-year-old, said to be ninety, with a face lined like crushed silk. She clambered about gamely on the boat's curved roof to get wood for the cooking fire and laughed at most things. Aziz and his mother shared a hookah, made from a coconut shell filled with water and polished black with handling. It had a wooden stem topped by a clay bowl, which held the tobacco and molasses mixture. They filled it with the gooey stuff, and a live charcoal was placed on it. The smoke was drawn through the stem, then through the water, by sucking hard on a hole drilled in the coconut.

While the grandmother needed the tobacco, as a drug, to keep the pain of her aching joints at bay, for Aziz it was a more sensual experience; he cradled the hard, polished wood of the coconut in one hand, and closed his eyes to draw the treacly smoke deep into his lungs. The hookah suffused his senses, he touched it as a lover might, and revelled in the sweet taste; even the sound of the smoke bubbling up through the coconut was the sound of water rippling past a boat. After the hookah, cigarettes tasted piffling, harsh and unpleasant.

Aziz's daughter, who told us her name was Shilpi, was performing a feat which can only have been possible after long practice. She sat on the prow, about two feet above the waterline, with one leg curled below her and the other knee raised, stretching down to rinse a cup in the river. Her head and shoulders were well below the level of her legs, but there was no apparent strain involved – a perfect adaptation to life on a boat. She was about ten, her hair was wildly out of control, and she looked like a witch, but went inside the boat to brush her hair, put on a dress, and to smudge pink lipstick round her lips as soon as Peter started to take photographs.

From time to time, as the money changed hands on the other boat, the gamblers offered Peter – who was wading about like a heron – and myself *pan* and tea, sending a servant off to the tea stalls quarter of a mile away to fetch it.

Aziz told us that his wife, Hena, was out touring the villages, selling bangles, combs, mirrors and crockery. She left, he said, early every morning and wouldn't return until it was nearly dark. His own business was in pink pearls, and he showed us a handful of the glowing, bud-like beauties.

'You must come tonight,' he said, inviting us to eat with them. 'It won't be a meal like you're used to ...' And he frightened himself with imagining what we might eat usually. 'What do you eat? Do you eat rice?

'Rice, yes.'

'Fish? Chicken? But not too hot.'

'No, no we like hot food.'

'But you're not used to it.'

'It's OK, we're used to it.'

His panic lessened.

When we returned to eat that evening it was hard to convince him that the meal was sufficiently rich or good. His wife, a woman of character, who talked even when her husband was talking, was less worried – she'd done the cooking, and knew it was good.

She explained that Bedeh women have traditionally traded through the villages, 'Strange men aren't allowed into house compounds, especially if the men are out in the fields during the day. If a strange man comes, who isn't a brother or close relation, then the women have to shut themselves away, to hide. But when we arrive, all the women gather. I tell them the news from beyond the village, and sell them things, bangles, mirrors, combs, crockery. If they let their husbands buy these things they'd be bound to get the wrong shape, colour or size.'

Women's lives in Bangladesh are secret, but they find out and know more than their men think. Many retain pre-Muslim practices and beliefs; to some extent excluded from religion by the practice of Islam, they have hung onto many Hindu, or pre-Hindu rituals and patterns of behaviour, and the women who do break out of their constricting surroundings are tough. Some remind me of those crusading Victorian ladies; they've had to fight every inch of the way, and be twice as intelligent, as clever as the men to reach the same position – so of course they don't take any nonsense.

The Bedeh, and Bedeh women in particular, occupy a special place in Bengali mythology. They're regarded with both fear and awe by the land-based, static, rural population, and myths about them abound. Rabindranath Tagore wrote a short story entitled *The Bedeh Girl*, and everyone we met was talking about a new film called *Josna, the Bedeh Girl*. This film had grossed so much money that the bank had been moved to the producer's office – because all cinema receipts in Bangladesh are in cash, in small notes and coins, and the risk of transporting such large amounts of money had grown unacceptable. A film critic friend thought that the film was popular because it supported women and the poor, and he gave as an example a scene in which Josna stands up to the king and calls him a liar. When we saw it the cinema erupted in cheering at this point. But the film's popularity may have had more to do with the sexiness of the actress who plays Josna.

The screenplay of *Josna, the Bedeh Girl* is based on an ancient Hindu story, and on a belief, which still exists in some of the remoter parts of the country, that the Bedeh can bring back to life someone who has died of snake-bite. A person who dies after being bitten by a snake is still sometimes placed on a raft of banana stems and loosed into the river, in the hope that Bedeh will find the body and bring it back to life.

When I asked Aziz about this belief he made a gesture of dislike, and muttering something about *sapurhee* changed the subject. I discovered later that the Bedeh are divided into caste or clan groups, who hold themselves aloof from one another. Aziz didn't belong to the caste of snake charmers, *sapurhee,* who make their cobras and tree snakes dance, who extract snake venom and who have an evil reputation. He didn't want to talk about them, and when we met some *sapurhee* later it was obvious that they were a different kind of people.

146

We ate inside the boat, by the light of a hurricane lamp, squashed in under the roof. The two children and the grandmother were asleep under a mountain of shawls and coverlets behind us, although granny wasn't so fast asleep that she didn't wake when the hookah was lit. It was a tight squeeze to fit us all in, but of necessity their possessions were neatly stowed along the sides of the cabin, which measured no more than ten feet by four. Aluminium and brass cooking pots were stacked one end, and were used as drawers, a couple of shelves held numerous glass bottles and jars for spices and other valuables, and Aziz kept his papers in an attaché case stored beneath a cassette player. Under the roof were two paddles, and a rice winnower.

They were good, relaxed hosts, and it was hard to credit the story we'd been told by a local Sylheti historian, a contact I'd been given in London. 'My niece,' he said, 'was talking to two Bedeh women selling the usual trinkets, and they somehow hypnotized or drugged her. She felt as though she was floating, as though nothing mattered. And then they persuaded her to give them all her gold jewellery. They were only prevented from getting away with this trick by the servant girl who fled to the next-door neighbours, shouting that the mistress had gone mad!'

Other people told us similar stories, but they may have had more to do with the perceived freedom, and therefore danger of the Bedeh than the truth.

Hena was a clever woman, and it was easy to imagine her running rings around most village people, whether educated or not, but she wasn't a thief. A nineteenth-century administrator wrote that the Bedeh 'amuse the villagers with tricks of jugglery, bear and monkey dancing, and when all else fails generally betake themselves to stealing,' and others assert that the Bedeh belong to a traditional robber caste.

The stories about Bedeh remind me of those told about the *hijra*, of the fear and contempt people feel for them because they represent the forbidden (and desired). *Hijra* are accepted in a particular place and at a particular time – at weddings and births – but they're still dangerous because uncontrolled and unpredictable. The Bedeh also are mysterious figures to the majority; they come and go without warning, the women are free of the usual constraints in a Muslim society, and they work with – or some of them do – snakes, symbols of danger and of power.

The *sapurhee* came up behind us on a path – three women, with snake baskets on their heads – and they demanded large sums of money to make one cobra perform. It was late afternoon, the sun was about to drop behind the trees, and we agreed a price quickly, so that Peter could take some photographs. No sooner had the most aggressive of the women put down her basket than a crowd formed, people coming out of nowhere and blocking the light. A truck came down the track and stopped, adding to the chaos; Peter was going quietly crazy. The woman squatted behind her basket and pulled out a large cobra. It wasn't interested in performing, shagged out perhaps after a long day of being charmed, or bullied, depending on how you look at it. She clenched her fist, waving it and undulating her forearm before the snake – it may have looked like another snake to the cobra. Occasionally she pulled its tail to liven it up a little. She chanted also, but it was the fluid movement of her hand and arm which interested the snake. It struck at her fist once or twice, and although she made no sudden movement and certainly didn't jerk away, her hand was never quite where it struck.

It was a tired snake though and while her attention was engaged by the camera it slipped away, into Peter's camera bag. She had to drag it out by the tail and treat it quite roughly to make it open its hood up again.

We'd wanted to be in Mymensingh by Christmas, and we spent days trying to find out how to get there by boat or on foot, but people either warned us against the idea, or said it was impossible in winter. The fishermen and bird fowlers who inhabit the vast marsh which spreads across northern Bangladesh were said to be wild and dangerous. The area was unpoliced – impossible to police anyway – and no one could tell us what it was like in the centre. We went out there, to the marsh, which stretched away to an horizon of hills. It was a confusing mass of inlets, streams, passages cut through the tall reeds which grew everywhere, and open water. It seemed unlikely that anyone could navigate their way all the way into Mymensingh district. The fishermen lived in reed houses on islands, and around the edge of the marsh. They certainly looked wild, although they were friendly enough, and claimed that they could do it, but it's about seventy-five miles to Mymensingh district, and without an introduction, patronage or protection it didn't seem like a good idea to entrust ourselves to them, especially as the journey in a sailing boat would take two or three days. Disappearances would be easy to arrange in a place like that.

We were stuck, but didn't want to have to return to Dhaka and then travel all the way north to Mymensingh, so our next idea was to try and cross the territory by a series of local river launches, the local bus of rural Bangladesh. Even this proved impossible, and we were still in Sylhet district when Christmas day dawned cold and misty. I stumbled off to the only tea shop in town which possessed an armchair (with cushion). The walls of the place, no more than ten feet square, were papered with newspapers – by chance from the time of the 1989 Tiananmen Square incident in Beijing.

Outside a second-hand clothes' salesman laid out four pieces of plastic on the ground, and then unpacked a bale of clothes. He himself dressed modestly, but the clothes he chose to sell were wildly extravagant – leopardskin velvet shirts, a silver lamé windcheater, fake-fur-lined, puce jackets, a fake sheepskin waistcoat. He didn't have to wait long for his first customer of the day. A rickshaw driver picked out a crushed velvet, plum-coloured shirt, and tried it on. Much to my disappointment he decided against it on the inadequate grounds that the sleeves were too long. Given such a garment, the vendor asked him, a once in a lifetime buy, what did the length of the sleeves matter? And anyway, look, you could roll them up.

The rickshaw driver had moved on, but Peter was waylaid as he came down the street, and he tried on a couple of things to amuse the Sylhetis.

The sun had dispersed the mist and cold by this time, and we decided to try and find a Tippra village nearby. A rickshaw took us through the Zafar Tea Estate, where a Union Jack drooped on a flagpole next to the Bangladeshi one – cheeky even for the zealous patriots in the tea trade, but perhaps the British High Commissioner was visiting for Christmas. A couple of tea garden workers saluted us as we went by, and in the distance, at the top of a nearby hill, stood the manager's house, an enormous low-roofed affair with a veranda the size of a tennis court, and purple bougainvillaea showering over it. Thinking about the managers' isolated lives in the past and even nowadays made me shiver. The tea gardens are managed as an extreme hierarchy: the managers live like gods, distant, unapproachable, and incomprehensible. Some even begin to believe that they are gods, that they can do exactly what they like.

A couple of years ago the owner of one garden was killed by his workers when he tried to cut their wages, and then blasted away at them with a shot-gun when they came to his house to complain. It's surprising that it doesn't happen more often.

We turned off the main road down a rough track made of broken bricks and sand, until the tea garden gave way to pineapples, planted up and down the hills like a parade of spiky troops. They scented the air with their clean, sharp smell. These in turn gave way to acres of the twisted and confused growth of lime trees, their thorny branches tangled together like barbed wire defences.

The rickshaw-able track came to an end and we stopped for a cup of tea in a wooden shack with hard benches and tables polished by a thousand elbows. The tea shop owner, assuming our generosity, gravely distributed cake to everyone present.

The path led on through the lime groves for a mile or so to where, at the top of a slight rise on a bend in a river, a group of Tippra had built some long, low mud and thatch houses. The lime groves stretched away on two sides, while the other two were open to the river, and areca nut trees protected the yard from the worst of the sun.

A woman was weaving a dark green cloth, with a wide red border and a few thin red stripes, on a backstrap loom tied to a house post. In the centre of the courtyard sat an old man, contemplating nothing. Three others were rebuilding or repairing the roof of one of the four houses.

When we arrived there was a slight, almost imperceptible stiffening, and my opening, involuntary remark, on the beauty of the place, did nothing to reduce it.

'What's so good about it?' asked one of the men, not, I think, meaning to sound aggressive, but for him it was just a place to live, and not a particularly good one.

They were polite, although they had no reason to be, producing a cane chair, and apologizing for not being able to offer us anything. They thought we were missionaries, and perhaps my opening statement had been a bit missionary-like. We did what we could to dispel this notion, but almost the only foreigners they'd seen were missionaries, and they didn't like them.

It was all too sudden anyway, and I wondered what I was doing there; it's not possible to turn up and expect to learn anything. I was just satisfying a vague curiosity, being voyeuristic again.

None the less I talked to the old man about the *jhum*, the shifting agriculture they used to practise, and he seemed to enjoy thinking about it, recalling it all as he sat in the sun with his useless legs stretched in front of him.

'Before the British time,' he said, 'there was so much land and space here, we never had any problems. Now there's nothing; we wear what we make, sell limes and eat what we can buy with the money it brings. Five years ago the river took our rice land, and now we have only the lime trees.'

In a few years, it was clear, the river would take the village too; there was nothing they could do in the long term, only delay it for a year or two by staking the bank.

The young woman abandoned her weaving at this point, and went into her house, driven away by our presence or my questions. The cloth lay abandoned and lifeless, half-finished; it hung from the post, half in the air and half on the ground. I could see the woman standing inside, in the shadow of the door, peering out through a crack.

It was too much, and I gave up, hating to disturb their lives, their day like this, for no clear purpose, and we left.

By the time we got back to Sri Mongol it was raining, and I sat disconsolately in a tea shop having a late lunch. Opposite me was an old man reading a newspaper. I hoped that he wasn't going to talk to me – I wasn't in the mood for the predictable questions – but he did.

'Excuse me, sir, but which part of the world are you from?' he said in perfect English.

It was a new way of phrasing the usual question and I perked up. He turned out to be a nonagenarian, who hadn't been back to Bangladesh for forty-two years. I asked him how he found it, and he didn't hesitate, 'It's no good, everyone's corrupt. It would be better if the British came back.'

'There's not much chance of that.'

'No, but still, whatever their faults and their cruelties, at least the place worked in those days. Now nothing works as it should. I'm going back to London in a few months, when it's warmer.'

His name was Kamal Rahman. He'd served in the British merchant navy during the Second World War, and had been torpedoed three times. The last time he was one of only three survivors from the merchant vessel, *Hulton Dean*, sunk in the Pacific by the Japanese. He'd been picked up and made a prisoner of war in Nagasaki. I must have looked disbelieving at this point in the story, because he said, 'Yes, yes, it's true. Three days before the Bomb went off we were transferred to a camp in Tokyo; the American officers knew something was going to happen, and they insisted that we should all be transferred.'

He had eleven children, mostly born in Britain. Wondering whether they faced the same problems as many Bangladeshi families – a strict father who wouldn't let his daughters go out – I asked whether his children were married.

'Yes, yes, they're all married to different nationalities: American, English, Welsh, Jordanian, Saudi and so on. I love it when all my grandchildren come and stay; they're all different colours, speak different languages and behave differently.'

'Don't you mind some of your daughters marrying non-Muslims?'

'Not at all. Why should I?'

151

I'd been put off by his beard, usually the symbol of someone who has made the trip to Mecca, the ultimate pilgrimage for a Muslim, so I asked whether he'd been there.

'No. I've been quite close, but never all the way there. To be honest, what's the point?'

A fat, lethargic-looking young man, grown sleek on easy living, sat down next to us and Mr Rahman whispered loudly about him. 'He's a *pir*, or supposed to be, but religion's got nothing to do with what these people do. He just wears a red turban and declares himself a saint. What's the point in that? Except to earn money.'

He'd travelled all over the world and spoke, he said, about twelve languages, none of them well – not even Bengali.

'Americans are no good. They treat blacks, I mean African people, very badly. They're rude and unpleasant, but New York's OK. London started to go downhill in about 1945 of course, but it's still the world's greatest city.'

I asked him about crossing into Mymensingh.

'Don't be crazy. You can't do it. You'll have to go to Dhaka and then take a bus north. But what are you doing here anyway? It's not everyday that one meets a compatriot in a tea shop.'

I told him that I was just travelling around, for no particular purpose, that I enjoyed Bangladesh, but he shook his head and laughed disbelievingly, 'No, no you're a journalist, or a writer.'

Time was running short. We'd wasted so much time trying to find a way across the country that we decided to cut our losses and go back to Dhaka, as everyone advised. In fact Peter would have to get back to London soon, and it seemed unlikely that he'd make it to the Madhupur Forest. I had no intention of leaving until my visa had expired.

When we reached Dhaka – a long train ride later – we went to the house Mukta shares with her family deep in the heart of the old city. She's a professional, but her room contains little to show that she's successful and well travelled: a bed and a dressing table with a few books and some make-up, not much else. The room is lit by a plain, unshaded light bulb, and in places the cream whitewash is flaking from the walls. Almost the only personal touch is a wicker basket, lying on the floor, overflowing with *shiuli* flowers. She collects the pretty, trumpet-shaped blossoms every morning from beneath the tree in the garden, and their scent fills her room. The *shiuli* tree flowers at night, and its delicate white and orange flowers fall as soon as the morning sun begins to warm the air. It flowers for three or four months, pushing out a mass of new blooms every evening, and it can catch you unawares at night; the sensual, rich scent, like an incarnation of desire, has occasionally pulled me up breathless on a city street.

Mukta is a quiet, thoughtful person, and unlike most Bangladeshi women who are brave enough to challenge their own society she doesn't come from a rich or privileged background. When I first knew her, just out of university, she was scared of being seen in my company, or on the back of my motorbike, by one of her myriad relations. She wasn't frightened any more, and I asked her who'd changed – her or her relations.

'Me of course. They're no happier about the way I live my life than they were, but there's not much they can do about it. I earn my own money, so the family can't tell me that I'm dependent on them and that I must therefore do what they say.'

Mukta managed to wrangle an invitation for Peter and myself to a New Year party at a big house in Gulshan, Dhaka's rich ghetto, where an enormous marquee had been erected over the entire garden, and wood fires lit at strategic places amongst the tables. New Year is a big event, an opportunity for the rich – foreigners and Bangladeshis alike – to show off their wealth, to consume conspicuously and to dress up.

At the party a small man, a Bengali with the same latent energy as Picasso, approached us, glass in hand. 'There are rumours that some of the political parties intend to stop this kind of extravagance next year by throwing smoke bombs over the walls.' The idea seemed to please him, and he grinned naughtily. 'Look at those Aga-Khanis,' he said pointing at three fat, ugly men in perfectly cut suits. 'They're businessmen, and cleverer than all us Bengalis put together. Come, let me introduce you to a few people.'

He started with an Afghani woman, one of the last of the Dhaka landowning families of royal Afghan descent, who told me proudly that her family no longer owned slaves, 'But of course the common people are so loyal that when I go to my father's house they want to bow down and touch my feet.'

Mukta cringed and laughed.

A man from the British Council, a birdwatcher and animal lover, was talking about the gibbons in the forest near Sri Mongol.

'If you go into the forest and give the male mating call then the females will come and display to you, open their legs.'

'Can you do it?' someone asked.

'Yes. The last time I did it a female with a baby, which she was hiding from her mate, displayed to me, until the male came down out of the canopy, hand over hand, like an express lift.'

A Bengali woman of spectacular beauty, dressed in a heavy green and gold silk sari, encouraged him to give a demonstration. 'Make the call now. Go on I'd like to hear what it sounds like.'

He didn't need to be asked twice, and he brought the whole party of three hundred people to a shuddering silence as the call rose through the chattering and talking, the clinking of glasses and plates and cutlery. It started at a low-pitched 'Oo-oo-oo-oo-oo', and climaxed at an orgasmic, drawn out, shouted 'Oooooo', before falling again through a waterfall of 'Ah-ah-ahs'.

The guests slowly resumed their conversations, and the woman in green began to talk about poverty in Bangladesh. She had several sympathetic things to say about the poor, but the British Council man stared at her grimly as she spoke, at her heavy gold necklace with a central diamond the size of my thumb nail. When she'd finished he said, 'Yes, you can talk like that with half the wealth of Bengal around your neck,' and brought the conversation to a stop for the second time.

She wasn't particularly embarrassed by the remark, but pulled her sari up to cover the gem.

Nearby a Bengali was shouting at a dramatic Bohemian figure in a black shawl with a shock of white hair – the Pakistani counsellor, 'You bloody fucking bastard, how can you work for Zia-ul Huq and then work for Benazir Bhutto and still call yourself an honest man?'

An Australian diplomat defended him, 'But that's what diplomats do.'

The Bengali turned on him also, 'So if a fundamentalist Christian dictator seized power in Australia tomorrow, instituted martial law, banned political parties, and made sex outside marriage a capital offence you'd go on representing your country I suppose?'

Nearby the diplomat's wife, the blonde star of Australian TV's political satire, *Fast Forward*, had drunk too many vodkas and was berating the Australian High Commissioner, 'You're so bloody old for God's sake . . .'

He agreed, diplomatically.

Mukta and I danced. Beside us a petite black girl in a bright red mini-skirt was playing with a drunk Bengali man, keeping him there with her languorous dancing, but somehow always avoiding his touch – not being in the place he thought she was in when he made a grab, or attempted to kiss her.

'West Ken., Olympia actually,' she said when asked where she was from. She was seventeen, worked in a store in Oxford Street, and had come to stay with an ex-school friend whose parents worked in Dhaka.

'So how do you find Bangladesh?'

'It's paradise. There's a party every night, and everyone tries to pinch your bum.'

At midnight the champagne came out.

13

Beggars' Banquet

One evening a week the grand façade of the Dhaka High Court is the backdrop to a fair; beggars, holy men, charlatans, pickpockets and Bengal's itinerant singers, the Bauls, gather by the mosque in front of the court building to be fed, to buy, to sell, to show themselves off or to perform.

The open area before the High Court, the *maidan*, is transformed for this event. It's lit by numerous kerosene lamps and fires, and their orange glow gives a warmth to sights which might be too gross by the light of day. There are lepers, cripples, and encephalitics, people who hardly looked like people – children and adults – medicine sellers, fortune tellers, naked Hindu *saddhu* holding iron tridents and looking fierce, and Muslim *pir*.

A young man almost forced me to sit down before an impressive *pir* who'd come from Ajmer in the Western deserts of India. He was perhaps sixty, and wore a black fez-like affair on his grey dreadlocks. Around his neck hung an eclectic collection of polished stone and bead necklaces, amulets and chains, while his white beard reached half-way down his chest. He spoke neither English nor Bengali, but the man who'd introduced me appointed himself interpreter, and insisted on translating into English, a language over which he had no command.

Fortunately the *pir* was a man of relatively few words, relying more on a penetrating stare, which he used on me when he realized that our interpreter was performing no useful function.

He looked deeply, and disconcertingly into my eyes for a while, and then, to my alarm, began to wriggle and squirm as though having a fit. In fact he was trying to force one hand deep down inside his white robes, and I watched in fascination as he fought his clothing, beard, beads and amulets, wondering what he was going to dig up. It took a long time, but he finally emitted a sigh, and from a pocket somewhere behind the matted beard the *pir* produced his visiting card – a rabbit would have been less surprising – which he gravely and kindly presented to me. On one side was his name, Syed Hussain Ali Chisty, in English and Bengali, and an address in Ajmer. On the other side was an indistinct black and white photograph, in which only his fez, stare and beard were visible.

Everyone had an idea, a song, a product or a deformity to sell, and the atmosphere was cheerful, even gay, like a fair. The crowd, eating peanuts and spitting shells in the dust, reacted to the hideously deformed and broken bodies strewn around them much as a Victorian crowd might have reacted to a freak show – with a mixture of frank, almost amused, disbelief, a little horror and much fascination.

The fair's dominant theme was business. Indeed, for one man I met justice itself was a matter of business, as I found out when I asked what he did for a living.

'I am a witness,' he answered proudly, with one hand on his chest.

Confused, and thinking he'd misunderstood the question, I asked what the case was about.

'Oh, any case,' came the easy reply.

I quickly abandoned him and went over to where a crowd had gathered around a young woman, a Baul, who had a curious deep-throated voice. She was singing to the accompaniment of a drum, some tiny brass cymbals and a couple of hand-held bells. She'd worked herself into an ecstatic trance; tears were streaming down her face, and her body was wracked, as though with pain. It was powerful stuff, and the emotion she was tearing from the people around her was palpable; many were weeping along with her.

Beside her sat an old man who was working himself into a trance. His eyes were closed and his whole body shook as he jerked himself violently back and forth, back and forth. No one else took any notice of him, all eyes were on the musicians who provided a constant rhythmic beat, and the singer.

As I watched the singer Mukta came and stood beside me. The lamps lit her gentle face, and the long hair piled loosely on her head; I was entranced.

The singer sang:

It is best to find a local love.
An outsider, a foreigner and a parakeet
Cannot be brought under control . . .

Dhaka draws its name, it is said, from a temple built where a statue of a Hindu goddess was found in the jungle: *Dhaka Iswari*, or 'Hidden Goddess'. Nothing remains of the temple, and there's now little to show that it was a great city of a million inhabitants when Calcutta was still only a village.

In the seventeenth century Dhaka's wealth astonished all visitors; even in a year when it had been pillaged by rebels it was able to send over two million rupees in specie to Delhi. This affluence was based on the skill of its weavers, who made a diaphanous muslin so fine that its like has not been seen before or since. Sixty yards of this material, reported the seventeenth-century traveller François Bernier, would fit in the palm of your hand, and in the Dhaka museum there is a turban, thirty feet long and three feet wide, which folds easily into a matchbox. A cloth of such luxury was much in demand, and it was bartered from Rome to Japan; every princeling had to have some.

The trade was brought to its knees by the British imposition of a tax on all local cloth – the better to sell Manchester piece goods – and collapsed completely as the old courts drifted into chaos with the growth in power and influence of Europe. By the beginning of the nineteenth century Dhaka could count only 50,000 inhabitants. 'The bones of the cotton weavers,' wrote the Governor General of the East India Company in a memorable phrase, 'are bleaching the plains of India.'

As Dhaka's population fell the jungle encroached on the city, and the East India Company's employees hunted tigers in the ruined, overgrown garden of the former Mughal Viceroy's palace.

The city has expanded again since then, and beyond what remains of the old city is a ring of developments; the British built a University, the High Court, a classic of Indo-Victorian architecture, and in the eighteenth century a cemetery.

The rich have moved out even further, to new housing estates where the streets are swept clean each morning, and every house has a garden full of flowering trees: frangipani, oleander and acacia.

There the shops are cluttered with tinned cheese, American rice and imported toys. Polished Mercedes and Nissans with even more polished chauffeurs, pack the streets. There is real money here, banked money, and most of it is stolen, or 'leaked' from the one billion dollars in aid Bangladesh receives each year.

The Sonargaon Hotel epitomizes this side of the city. It is new, Japanese, and expensive. From the outside it looks like a jail, or a missile silo; nothing but blank concrete walls. Inside it is a wonder of space, white marble and fountains, and all its windows look inwards.

The traffic wasn't so much jammed as locked into place – as though a giant hand had squeezed the mass of buses and rickshaws together, welding them into a piece of 'found' sculpture, a mess of chrome, paint and exhaust fumes, through or over which a hundred thousand people were trying to make their way.

Mukta and I had planned a gentle day in the countryside – Peter had already left – and being stuck in traffic for two hours with air horns exploding the pollution-laden atmosphere every few seconds wasn't a good start. Our bus was an old Bedford; it was decorated inside with dusty plastic flowers, fairy lights which flashed on and off, and a few edifying proverbs: 'Your behaviour shows your family background'. There were also instructions to watch your pockets, and not to lean out of the windows.

A man pushed up to where we sat and rubbed his groin against Mukta's shoulder, while he looked the other way. She complained loudly and he retreated slightly, surprised that she wasn't too embarrassed to say anything. Another passenger, in a Muslim skull-cap, who was standing nearby, remonstrated violently with the first man, and he removed himself entirely. For the remainder of the journey the man in the cap protected Mukta from other frustrated, predatory males, shaming them into moving away, or at least not breathing down her neck.

Part of the problem was that she was sitting with me towards the rear of the bus. She refused to sit in one of the few, uncomfortable, cramped places next to the driver which are reserved for women, saying that it was the most dangerous place on the bus.

Fifteen miles outside Dhaka we climbed out, and took a rickshaw into the countryside. The machine crashed and rattled, at little more than walking pace, over the dried mud track, past fields of paddy, beneath flowering trees and enormous bamboo stands. Apart from our transport and the birds the world was silent. After a while we got down, and leaving the rickshaw we wandered across the fields, and round the edges of square, man-made ponds, from which the earth had been used to construct platforms for homesteads. In the monsoon everything but these platforms would be covered in a sheet of water, unless it was a bad year and the rivers rose too high.

A Shiva temple stuck up out of a clump of bamboos beside a river, where a fisherman raised a counter-weighted, triangular net from the water and grasped a handful of silver slivers, putting the fish carefully into the folds of the lungi which was tied up around his loins.

It was cool among the bamboos and we sat there, watching a group of naked children, like tiny, black froglets, leaping off the bank, swimming in the muddy river, and fighting over a rowing boat. They all had short, cropped hair, and apart from their nose studs the girls were indistinguishable from the boys once they were in the water. A woman and her teenage daughter stopped on their way to the pond to get water, to talk to us. They were Hindu, she told us; her husband's family had been *zamindar,* big landowners. She pointed at the ruins of a house through the bamboos, smoke drifting up from within its broken walls. 'It was destroyed by the Pakistanis during the Liberation war in 1971. The image of Lord Shiva was stolen from this temple at the same time.'

The woman kept wrapping her cheap, print sari round herself and over her hair, pulling it tight, and fiddling with the end which hung down beside her head – the infinitely adaptable sari, revealing or concealing only so much as is desired at the moment, and providing a constant source of activity for nervous hands. Her daughter was more self-possessed, had been more exposed to influences beyond the village perhaps.

One of the little girls in the boat, in a fit of fury because her brother wouldn't give her the oar, grabbed his shorts from the bottom of the boat and flung them into the water. The boy retrieved them, and thumped the girl before leaping back into the river. She screamed and cried, but soon recovered enough to pick up his shorts again, jump from the boat onto the bank and run off, hotly pursued. The boy caught her in a hundred yard sprint and started to administer a serious bashing, but he was interrupted by a large, fat man who held them apart, and made them shake hands before proceeding calmly on his way.

Mukta and the woman fascinated each other. The life of the one was incomprehensible to the other, to such an extent that the woman asked Mukta whether she was a Bengali or a foreigner, which received an indignant response.

'A Bengali, of course, do I look like a foreigner? Do I speak Bengali like a foreigner?'

'Well no, but . . .'

She couldn't figure us out. She knew I was English, and she'd already established that Mukta was a Muslim, and this combination didn't make any sense to her. 'How many children do you have?'

'I don't have any,' Mukta replied, not answering the real question, which was whether I was her husband.

The woman left us to her daughter who was determined to show us a

Hindu *saddhu*, a holy man who, she assured us, lived in a tree. It sounded too good to be missed.

'The *saddhu* lives just down here, in those trees you can see beside the river. He can walk on water, and is very fierce,' the girl said with excitement.

We walked beside the Meghna, miles wide although it's a hundred and twenty miles from the sea, dotted with islands and with beds of mauve water hyacinth floating downstream. The sun was setting spectacularly into the horizon of water, and the air was still. There was a sense of elemental immensity about the landscape – sky, water and land – flat and painted in plain colours.

The two trees in which the *saddhu* lived were enormous; they covered so much ground that they constituted a forest by themselves, and sent down an array of roots from their thick branches. Leaving our shoes outside we stepped over a low bamboo fence, into the shadow, and peered timidly into the leafy branches, expecting to see a monkey maybe, or a real man, with orange robes and matted hair, probably driven a little crazy by his life in a tree.

'Come on, let's look at him,' the girl said, leading the way towards two huts deep in the shade.

There was an ominous silence, not a leaf stirred, and outside in the sunlight the river spread like a plain. I couldn't help looking upwards fearfully, half-expecting someone to leap out at us waving a trident at any moment. The girl walked up to one of the huts and stood beside it.

'He's in here. Open the door.'

Mukta told her she could have the honour (I was craven enough to have retreated some distance, ready to flee), so the girl crept closer and with great drama pushed the door, which swung inwards on its bamboo hinges.

'Come and look,' she whispered.

We tiptoed up, wonderingly. Images of *saddhu* who haven't moved in twenty years came to mind, of ones who've held one arm above their heads for half a lifetime, until the muscles and flesh have withered, leaving only a dry, skeletal stick, and wildly twisted nails a foot long.

Mukta let out a laugh, and relaxed, pointing. On the mud floor of the hut sat the *saddhu*, cross-legged, bearded and benign. He'd been dead twenty-five years, and a white plaster image had taken his place.

We returned to Dhaka, and I bought a ticket in advance for a bus going to Mymensingh. Before I went north though, Mukta was determined I should meet an old political fire-eater, a Hindu lawyer. He'd been one of the framers of, and signatories to independent Bangladesh's first Constitution, and at different times he'd been Bangladesh's Ambassador to Japan, and the country's Finance Minister.

More importantly he had been a revolutionary all his life. Mukta didn't know him, but was convinced that he'd be an interesting man to talk to.

When I turned up unannounced he greeted me a little warily – as politicians are wont to greet writers or journalists, announced or not. I was shown into a high-ceilinged reception room, where the cream whitewash had faded. The decoration consisted of pictures of Rabindranath Tagore, Jesus Christ (a particularly lurid sacred heart one), Mahatma Gandhi spinning, the Bengali, revolutionary poet Nazrul Islam, and Sheikh Mujib, the founder and first president of independent Bangladesh. Three nondescript calendars (one showing Nelson's Column) filled in some of the larger empty spaces on the walls. Otherwise the room was bare, apart from a glass case containing an elaborately dressed Japanese doll, a princess, done out in an immense quantity of finery and silk. It was an odd symbol for a revolutionary to have brought back from Japan, or to have been given.

He'd been born in what was then East Bengal in 1903, and had, he said, 'joined politics' at the age of thirteen – six years later he was imprisoned for the first time by the British, and in total he'd spent twenty years of his life in jail, during both the British and the Pakistani times. Three years had been spent in solitary confinement under the British who, he said, 'Merely mistreated me in the prison in the Rajputana desert, whereas the Pakistanis tried to destroy me.'

He talked about his failing health as a result of the years in jail, but he looked a spry sixty, rather than the eighty-seven he was. His eyes were bright and he moved without apparent difficulty; he was still a well-built man, with no suggestion of fat. His fine, white hair was brushed down close to his small round head. On the slightly hooked, Brahminical nose was balanced a pair of heavy black-framed glasses. The most remarkable thing about him was the lack of lines on his face. Apart from the deep scores which ran from the sides of his nose to his immobile mouth, he had no more lines than you'd expect to find on the face of a thirty-year-old.

It was the eyes which gave him away – ignoring them I could imagine him, under different circumstances, being a friendly old tea shop owner – but they were shrewd, assessing eyes, those of a politician, and they marked him out as a hard man, someone who didn't miss anything.

He wasn't interested in, and was unwilling to answer, my questions, but gave me a lecture, a run down on his life, starting in 1922 when he'd first been thrown in jail by the British. He'd fought for independence from Britain, and had been released from jail in 1947 only six weeks before Independence was due. 'Brother, I didn't sleep for those six weeks, I travelled all over East Bengal campaigning for the elections, and it paid off because I was elected to the East Pakistan Legislature.'

He hadn't married until he was well into his forties because politics had taken up all his time, and his first sight of his first child was in 1952, from the window of a train taking him to jail, 'Because I had foreseen that a Bangladesh independent from Pakistan was an inevitability, and had said so.'

His grandchildren played in the garden outside while he talked, the rumbling sound of spices being ground by hand came from the kitchen, and the ringing of an occasional rickshaw bell entered through the windows which opened onto the lane. His wife brought tea and biscuits twice during the three hours I listened to him; she was still a good-looking woman whose gold-rimmed specs gave her a studious, youthful air.

He had clashed with Gandhi over the issue of violence, but whenever the Mahatma's name, or the names of his other political colleagues and friends came up – and there were many of them – he was silent for a few moments as though honouring their memory.

'My mind is burning when I think of what is happening now, when I look at the present political situation ...' he said, and this woke in him the old fire, his voice rose and he asked rhetorical questions (the silences which followed made me nervous). He shouted and then talked quietly and confidentially – I was forgotten, he was addressing a crowd – and I could see how he must have had them eating out of his hand.

When the story of his life was over I asked whether he was still a revolutionary.

'Yes,' he replied without hesitation, 'I am still a revolutionary because history is on the side of the revolutionary.'

There was something glorious in an eighty-seven-year-old saying this, and pointing dramatically at the picture of Gandhi he continued, 'After all, he was the greatest revolutionary of them all, and he was right wasn't he?'

14

Peacock, Tiger and Pig

'Excuse me sir. You are American I think.' The man had managed to grab the seat next to me the moment it was vacated – there was stiff competition for seats among the hundred or so passengers travelling on the bus to Jolchotro in the Madhupur Forest.

'English.'

'From London perhaps?'

I nodded.

'I am going to Manchester in London in three weeks' time to study a course on veterinary medicine. England is the most civilized and developed country in the world.'

'It's not that good.'

He affected surprise. 'But a friend from my home town has written to me from Edinburgh in London that we are living in a jungle in Bangladesh. Those were his words; he wrote that Bangladeshis are jungle-livers, that we are most uncivilized people. It's not possible for a savage living in a jungle to be civilized.'

He didn't really believe that what he was saying referred to Bangladeshis, it was just a conversational gambit; it's easy to be charmed by people who run themselves and their country down, and Bangladeshis are past masters at that particular game.

I argued that people we call savages are often more civilized than the rest of us – they behave decently to each other, rarely steal and tend to have strong ideas about lying.

'But as mankind is the highest creation of Allah, or of your God, then ...'

'I don't believe that ... I think mankind is the lowest, most uncivilized creation.'

He was thunderstruck. 'No, that is not possible; the order of the universe leads upwards towards mankind.'

'What order? The nature of the universe is random – there's no static order, it changes according to a million variables.'

'Even so the happiest people are pious ones.'

I couldn't follow the logic of this but asked whether he therefore believed that the Sharia, or Islamic law, should be introduced – to make everyone happy.

He replied evasively, 'Without laws we are animals.'

'Animals are superior to us,' I countered. 'They don't murder, steal or lie. Nor do they have religion. Religion is fundamentally irrational, but if you believe in Islam you might as well go the whole way and argue for the introduction of the Sharia.'

I was, I admit, getting a little carried away.

'Yes, it should be introduced, but the government would not implement the laws – they don't implement the laws which exist now.'

The other passengers were beginning to take an interest in our discussion – the ones who could hear relaying the story down the bus, and adding their own comments above the rattling, the choking, and the rumbling of the ancient chassis over a severely pot-holed road.

My neighbour went on, 'The government might introduce the Sharia, but these people,' and he gestured at the peasants strap-hanging over us, 'these people would never obey.'

The passengers grinned, and looked pleased with themselves, and only then did I realize that we'd gone past Jolchotro. I shouted and banged on the side of the bus, and after half the passengers had taken up the cry we came to a juddering halt.

My bag was thrust out through a window, and fell to the ground with a thud. I disembarked with difficulty as it entailed everyone else disembarking also, so tightly were they packed. Once they'd squeezed themselves back in and the bus had rumbled off in a cloud of black exhaust, there was silence and stillness, apart from the rustle of leaves in one of the great trees arching over the road. It seemed odd that greenery should be snowing down from above and I glanced up, to see a family of rare golden langurs stripping the tree, eating only the stems and negligently dropping the rejected leaves. They had black faces and long black tails, white ruffs around their faces, and lovely, rufous chests.

The Mandi, who inhabit the Madhupur Forest, were the first mountain people with whom the rulers of Bengal came into contact as they tried to extend their domination eastwards. Early British records mention them frequently, usually as 'a truculent, obstinate people, much given to harrying the plains'. The Mandi had held out in the Garo Hills, the outermost end of the mountain promontory which runs into the rice lands of Bengal, against the British, for longer than any other group.

They'd regularly conducted raids on the plains' villages which fringe the hills, asserting that they'd originally owned or controlled these villages, and they were greatly feared, perhaps not surprisingly. According to one source they used to fill the reeking, decapitated heads of their victims with food and drink, and have a party – but the Rev. W. Carey was writing fifty years after the events he described, and as a missionary he had an interest in exaggerating the former wildness of the people he was working among.

Not until a punitive campaign in 1866–7 did the Mandi fall under the sway of the queen empress, although the final resistance wasn't put down until 1873.

Late at night I was driven through the jungle by a Mandi friend, Sebastian, on his moped, to a wedding celebration. The path was everyone's but a motocross enthusiast's nightmare, and we slipped and slid all over the place. We knew when we were near because we ran into a group of drunk, red-faced Mandi staggering along carrying a great earthenware pot, containing beer, strung between two bamboo poles.

There was hardly a sober person at the wedding, although the Mandi there were all Baptists – supposedly strict teetotallers. The party was in the central courtyard of a square of mud houses, and a kind of tent of banana leaves had been erected to keep the sun off during the day. The oldest relation had a special place in the middle, and had to have the first glass from each pot of alcohol. He'd been at it for twenty-four hours, but looked pretty well considering. He was a big, solid fellow, and not the kind of person to take any nonsense from anyone; after I was introduced he dismissed me with, 'Well, he doesn't speak Mandi, and I don't speak English or Bengali, so that's that.'

Beer was forced down my throat, quite literally, a Mandi custom I later discovered. In his *Descriptive Ethnology of Bengal*, published in 1872, E. T. Dalton describes how, at a Mandi celebration, attendants with gourd bottles full of this homebrew, known as *chew*, poured it down the throats of the guests who had nothing to do but to sit still and open their mouths, 'as young birds in a nest open their mouths when the old birds return from foraging for them'. Dalton also describes how 'Some Mandi chiefs appear to live entirely on beer ... when they take it to this extent it is thickened with flour of millet, which makes it more nourishing, and though it keeps them in a perpetual state of "mild but sweet ebriety", they get fat on it.'

A man, who said he was a teacher, stumbled up to me and told what sounded like an old Mission story. 'In the time of Rani Victoria, a long time ago, an Englishman went to London to apply for permission to kill the wild beasts in her forest here – he meant us, the Mandi. As the great Rani was about to sign the paper an old pastor stood up and said, "Hang on a tick, let me go and see if these things are really animals or not." Rani Victoria dropped her gold pen and said, "That's a good idea, and go with my blessing".

'The pastor came to the jungle and with much cunning he caught a Mandi, washed him, because in those days we didn't wash, cut his hair, because we kept our hair long, and made him wear clothes, because we used to be naked. To his amazement the pastor found that the thing everyone thought was an animal could learn how to read and write, how to speak English, and even how to drive a car.

'After three years the pastor returned to England where he told Rani Victoria that the Mandi were humans not animals, so she said, "OK, go back and give them religion".'

Apart from the obvious 'Before and After' (Evident Benefits of Christianity) moral the story illustrated, for me, the importance and influence of the Mission in Mandi culture.

It was well after one in the morning when we left, and the teacher decided to join us, so it was three up through the jungle on a Honda 50. The raised track was no more than a foot wide, and because Sebastian forgot to switch on the headlight (neither of his two passengers noticed) it was difficult to negotiate. Half-way through the forest, where the track divided and widened out, Sebastian and the teacher had an argument about which was the right way. As they waved their arms about we all fell off. Once we'd righted ourselves and the machine we were off again, churning through the sand, using up the entire width of the track, until we reached the road, which was blanketed in thick, cold fog.

'If we get through this bit then we're OK,' said Sebastian encouragingly as we rode at walking pace down the side of the road.

Thinking that we'd been through the worst I unwisely asked why.

'Because this is where the bandits are.'

No bandits appeared, although we would have been a push-over. It wasn't until the next morning that we heard we'd driven within a few yards of a body, of someone who'd been killed by bandits earlier and whose corpse hadn't been found until the morning.

A day later news of another attempted murder came: a Mandi had been stabbed and robbed quarter of a mile away on his way back from the market, where he'd sold his buffalo. It was touch and go whether he was going to live. The bandits, I was told, always struck on market days.

Their victim did survive this time, and I met him when he came out of hospital. He was a tough old man, pure muscle and moustache, and he was in a fury, determined to get his own back on both the bandits, because he knew who they were, and on the Forest Department Guards. The guards, who are armed, were implicated not only because they'd stopped him on his way to the market and asked whether he was going to sell the buffalo, but also because they'd been hanging around in the trees when he was robbed – so they'd obviously taken a cut.

Someone else explained that the old man and his friends would set a trap for the bandits, and kill them. It was just a question of time.

The law in Bangladesh is so corrupt, and so weighted against minorities that the Mandi often take it into their own hands, although they have a great number of traditional laws themselves. The British codified Mandi law, recognizing the system as superior to anything they might have been able to replace it with. Crimes under Mandi law include 'winking with intent at a woman', the point being that it's the woman who should make the first move, not the man. Another law makes it an offence for a man to touch a woman's breasts while she's lying down, or in a position which makes it hard for her to defend herself. If the woman doesn't care for such an approach she can take the man to the village court.

On the other hand marriage by capture used to be the rule. Father Homrich, the Catholic priest who's lived at Jolchotro for twenty-five years, said that it still went on. It's usually the woman who captures the man, not the other way round. That is to say that her male friends do it for her. In the early days the missionaries would rush to the rescue, thinking that violence was being done, but they learnt that the shouting and struggling was all part of the show.

'Most people sleep together before they're married.' For a Catholic priest Father Homrich was very relaxed about this. 'The Mission operates as a sort of refuge for all sorts of people: Muslim women from their husbands, and Mandi girls from their clan. If a Mandi wife dies then her husband has the right to take one of her younger sisters, but the girls are far too sensible nowadays; they want to finish their education and choose their own husband rather than marry some dirty old man, so they run away. Many elope to the Mission also, whether they're Catholic, Baptist, Anglican or Sangsarek – traditional pagans – and they usually have what's known as a "blanket marriage".'

Father Homrich was a little cagey about this term, but when I pressed he responded shortly. 'The couple is covered with a blanket and they're considered married.'

Mandi law also treats it as attempted murder if someone takes a *dao*, and while shouting an incoherent account of injuries received at another's hands, expressing a desire for revenge and naming the adversary, slices through a banana tree with a single stroke.

I spent many hours going through Father Homrich's collection of books on the Mandi – I even found a translation of *Ben Hur* in Achik, one of the many Mandi languages. The words were so delightful that I copied down the opening paragraph: '*Dal,dalbegipa Asia, Africa, aro Europe a.songrangko nangrimatgipa chonbegipa ku,rachakgimin A.songo gita ia a.gilsakni biapo bano an.chi pakaha ...*' One word in particular caught my attention for its sound, it was *tingtotprakna*, and Sebastian translated it for me; it was a metaphor and meant 'to throw water at one another', in other words, to blame each other.

Father Homrich is deeply involved in human rights' issues in the area. He said that he would die there, and seemed to think that he might be murdered one day. The Mandi had tried to poison him once, but that was many years ago, before they saw him as an asset in their fight with the majority society. Now if anyone murdered him it would be the Forest Guards, or local Bengali politicians, or businessmen, or government ministers who are making money by selling off the Mandi's land and trees.

The Mandi village I stayed in was deep in the forest, and it was one of the prettiest places I've ever seen. The house had thick mud walls, and consisted of a courtyard surrounded on three sides by a raised, stamped-mud veranda. Wooden pillars supported the roof, and the rooms led directly off this veranda. The fourth side of the courtyard was closed by a wooden grain storage barn, set on stone pillars. There were flowerbeds round all four sides of the courtyard, and they were filled with marigolds, asters, dahlias large enough to sweep the board at any village show in England, sixteen different kinds of rose, a white jasmine which climbed up over the house, and many other, more exotic plants. When the sun was low it projected the shadows of bamboo leaves onto the warm coloured mud walls of the house.

At the rear of the house were outbuildings: the kitchen, a wood store, and sleeping quarters for the men who worked for my host. In the early evenings the place looked like a picture in a children's book, in which there are too many things happening at once: two cocks fighting, two piglets slurping up food, three men sawing a tree into planks, one man turning hay, two women cooking and another making puffed rice on a fire outside, a daughter collecting water from the hand-pump, a couple of dogs sleeping, and the head of the household wandering serenely about, shrewd as anything.

'You wouldn't believe the trouble we had getting the piglets here,' my host said. 'They couldn't travel in the bus like goats or chickens because they're unclean to Muslims, and in fact we had to hide them in a big basket. Then the porters refused to carry the basket because they found out what was in it, and when we did persuade one he wanted ten times the normal price. It was a nightmare.'

I spent the most of my time talking to the man's sister, Kohima, who was fascinated by the idea of travel, and believed that I must be rich to be able to afford it. Each evening we had long discussions on the nature of wealth; I failed to convince her that in real terms she was more wealthy in her own right than I am. She was tough, intelligent and lovely, and had recently been attacked by some forest guards who'd started to pull up her pineapple crop on the grounds that it was planted on government land. This was untrue, and she showed me the papers to prove it; it was just another example of harassment. Her arms, shoulders and head were still badly bruised from the beating. To add insult to injury they'd then charged her with assault – there'd been six of them and one of her.

The family were Catholics, and over my bed was a picture of Pope John Paul II in full regalia, rising like a giant above a painting of the Vatican, one finger raised in admonition. Talking to Kohima it became clear that Christianity has become a profession; the brightest boys, those who want to get on, to travel and to earn a decent living, join the Church, or get a job with one of the Christian charities.

In the evenings the family, their three Bengali workers, two dogs, a cat called Dulu, or Dust, and myself, gathered around a fire outside wrapped in shawls, to talk, play *karom*, a kind of board-billiards, or to stare into the embers. It wasn't a static group: the dogs would get up to bark at the night, the children would rush off to gather shavings and fling them on the fire with screams of delight, the men to find cigarettes and the women to prepare food. While the women worked, the Mandi men discussed Church matters, and the constant battles which rage between Mandi Baptists, Catholics and Anglicans. I heard stories of villages and families divided by the minutiae of Christian theology, and of parents forbidding or refusing to attend marriages.

Ecumenicalism has not reached into the forest.

It was there, sitting round the fire under the stars, that Kohima told me of an important demon who'd died a long time ago. 'At his funeral,' she said, 'a great number of buffaloes had to be sacrificed in his honour, but while they were being driven *en masse* to the slaughter they were disturbed by the noise of the funeral drums and the mourners' wailing. Frightened, they stampeded, making the star track across the sky.' The Milky Way.

She apologized for not being able to offer me any alcohol but, 'We drank it all over Christmas and the New Year, and the new brew isn't ready yet.' She grew conspiratorial, and added, 'Bengalis often buy alcohol from us, but sometimes we lace it with juice made from the root of a particular kind of gourd, which is a hallucinogen; the Bengalis think they've got drunk on one glass, when in fact they've been poisoned. It doesn't kill them, just makes them feel bad for a few days.' And she laughed unroariously.

Occasionally picnic parties of Bengalis would come into the forest in buses, loudspeakers blaring, destroying the peace, and Kohima described how they got rid of them. 'We go up wind of the party and open the pods of a jungle flower very carefully. The seeds drift downwind into the bus or into the group, and in a few minutes they're all jumping,' she laughed. 'This seed makes you itch unbearably – so we sit there giggling while they tear at their clothes thinking they're being attacked by insects. They go pretty quickly after that.' She was worried that I'd misunderstood. 'If they didn't make so much noise and mess we wouldn't mind – but they've got no appreciation of where they are. They get drunk, annoy us women, get into fights and generally cause trouble, so the best thing to do is to get rid of them.'

I wanted to meet someone who followed the traditional Mandi religion, Sangsarek, and one of the sons agreed to take me to a village where there were said to be followers of Sangsarek. When we reached the village we stopped at several houses with Sangsarek death posts outside – anyone who dies is commemorated with a carved wooden post, which informs those who can read about the dead person. The people in these houses all said that the posts were old, and that they themselves were Christians. Only in one house was the grandfather Sangsarek, but he was in a drunken sleep, so we couldn't talk to him.

Finally we came to a house which the family was busy rebuilding. They'd taken the thatched roof down, and had knocked away the walls; now they were reconstructing them. One man collected great dollops of red clay from the river, and dumped it in the place where the wall was going to be, and another patted it into cuboid sections. As it dried it cracked, so the last phase was to fill in the cracks and give a clean, plaster-

171

like finish inside and out with another kind of mud mixed with cow dung.

The family weren't unwilling to talk about being Sangsarek, and they all stopped work to rest in the shade and chat. They explained that the children went to school so they'd become Christians, but they didn't find this odd or difficult, and said that people sometimes changed back to Sangsarek when they got old. They couldn't really tell me much about their religion, and the grandmother suggested that I should ask Father Homrich, that I'd learn more from him than I would from them.

I decided to leave the village and to walk to the Mission through the forest, rather than going round it on a less interesting path. Kohima warned me that the track was infested with bandits, but I was determined to do it anyway.

I met an old Mandi woman carrying a tree on her head; a man on a bicycle who greeted me with the words 'Hello Father', in English (I made the sign of the cross, incorrectly, and muttered some dog Latin, which was all I ever knew); three barefoot Muslim women in a line, the first two concealing their faces behind their saris as they passed, and the third, the youngest, peeking with big eyes from a dark face, but hiding quickly when I smiled (probably lecherously); a group of tiny girls on their way to school, dressed in blue, who, chattering like parakeets, stopped, turned towards me, raised their hands to their foreheads, palms together, and said 'Namushkar' in unison, then continued sedately on their way; and seven villainous types holding assorted axes and *daos*. One felt the blade of his weapon and grinned at me wolfishly. They were woodcutters, but they gave me a nervous moment. A *dao* is not a pleasant-looking tool: it's large, for a start, and it has a steel blade, jagged in places, where it's been used to cut down trees, with darker, rust-like patches towards the thick top side. A *dao* is the colour of light streaming into a forest, or water over pebbles. It balances at the point where the blade joins the wooden handle, and it's sold by weight – fifty *taka* per kilo. It's silent until it strikes something solid. A *dao* can take off a buffalo's head in one blow; I've seen it happen so fast that the body of the shaggy beast continued to stand there stupidly while the blood pumped out in a jet, and the head lay on the ground. Then the legs collapsed and the thing became just meat. I wondered whether a human body could still stand after it had lost its head – there can't be many people who know the answer to that, dead or alive. A *dao* has other advantages: it doesn't require a licence, and it doesn't wear out. A *dao* is an affordable, essential accoutrement, one which swings handily, looks good and is a practical aid to eating, working, and resting – you can, for instance, pick your teeth with the point.

I also saw a mongoose, some pigeons, a flock of parrots, some other, brightly coloured but unidentifiable birds, and a troupe of langurs who threw leaves at me from the tops of the high *sal* trees, their trunks smooth as stone columns. Otherwise the walk was uneventful, and I arrived at the Mission a few hours later.

Sebastian had two suggestions. The first was that we go on his moped to watch the preparations for a Sangsarek ritual called Sushumi Amma which would be held the following day in a nearby village. He admitted that he himself had never seen it, although it was a common enough event. The second was that we go north to the border, an eight-hour trip by moped, to a Mandi Cultural Centre set up by the government.

'Why by moped and not by train?'

'Because foreigners are stopped on the train and in the bus. There's a revolutionary political party which controls, or semi-controls, much of the area, and the government doesn't want foreigners to know.'

I asked about the Cultural Centre, and the more I heard the less I liked the idea.

'The teachers are nearly all Bengali, although it's supposed to be a way for us, the Mandi, to keep in touch with our own culture. The dance teacher, for example, is a Bengali, and doesn't know anything about Mandi dance, so what he teaches is Bengali dance mixed up with a few misunderstood Mandi dance steps. The suggestion is always that Mandi culture is just a poor relation of Bengali culture.'

There wasn't much point in making such an arduous journey for so small a return, but the Sushumi Amma sounded like a different thing altogether. It was being held to aid the recovery of an old woman who'd been ill, and it was to be an expensive event, requiring at least two days' preparation, and much bamboo, drink and sacrificing. Sixteen men were busy cutting and decorating a stockade of bamboo when we arrived. They used their *dao* to cover the bamboos in zigzag patterns, to tassel them, and to make strips for a mat. They knew bamboo and knew their tools so well that they worked automatically. I watched one man splitting a six-foot length of bamboo; it was no more than two millimetres thick, but he split it into two strips one millimetre thick without bothering to look at what he was doing. The atmosphere was industrious and serious, without being glum – they were involved in what they were doing, as men are when they work. Apart from creating these bamboo representations of the gods some of the men were making a shelter, overlaid with banana leaves, to protect the guests from the sun.

We went back the next morning at eleven, to find that the sacrifices –

three pigs and thirteen chickens – had already been made. There was blood all over the bamboo stockade, daubed over it rather than sprinkled. Most noticeably the previously white, tasseled beards on the bamboos representing the gods Saljong and Sushumi had turned scarlet.

Most of the guests were already drunk. They forced *chew* down my throat as before, and produced pork cooked in various ways; I tried to eat slowly, but they piled more onto the banana leaf plate in front of me irrespective of what I said. The only person who was moderately sober was the Sangsarek priest, who sat on a stool at one end of the shelter chanting all the while. People occasionally took up the drums, cymbals and large, bowl-shaped gongs, and played. A group of six old women danced, while being stroked by the priest with a white cock's feather. In fact they didn't dance so much as turn in a tight circle around one of their number, and bent their knees, very slightly, in time with the music.

By late afternoon it was a bit difficult to keep track of what was happening. The party was collapsing.

Sebastian lurched up, and we leant against a house wall in the sun. 'The first stage of drunkenness,' he said, raising a finger, 'is the peacock, when the drinker is beautiful and dances beautifully to please himself. Then comes the second stage, the tiger, when everything and anything is possible.' He growled like a tiger, and we collapsed in giggles. Then he grew serious, 'The final stage is the pig, when there's nothing left but being sick, shitting and sleeping.'

The priest passed us and we stumbled after him, back to the stockade, where a chicken's throat was cut, its entrails examined and pronounced over, before it too was cooked. The old woman who'd been ill – and in respect of whose recovery the event was being staged – climbed into the stockade and was stroked with more feathers, yanked from the hapless chicken before it was killed. The priest drew lines with a piece of chalk down the spine and along the limbs of a black kid. It was lifted into the air and a man built like a galley slave chopped its head off with an old, two-handed Mandi sword.

More was eaten and drunk; I had to go for a walk to avoid it. I couldn't have eaten anything else without throwing up, but I didn't feel I was at the pig stage. Everyone was waiting for the *grigha*, which meant, I was told, the noise the Mandi make before a battle. When it started they all stood up – some of the men were big fellows, and I could imagine that it would be frightening to face them in battle. There was a fairly incoherent sounding of cymbals, drums, gongs and trumpets made of buffalo horns, a tremendous din. The priest stood too and grabbed a Mandi sword and shield. He danced around one end of the shelter, taking neat little steps, and struck at the banana leaf roof a couple of times, frightening the children who peered in from behind their mothers' backs.

When the priest put down the weapons I expected more drama, but he reached up, took down a pair of flip-flops from the roof, where he'd put them for safe-keeping, and walked quickly away.

It was the signal for the party to start in earnest, and I was dragged to my feet by a group of dancers, who hung one of the heavy drums around my neck, and laughed at my attempts to get a decent sound out of it. No one cared what uncoordinated movements I made, the point was to leap and jump as much as you could without falling over.

I left a couple of hours later and the Mandi were still revelling under the stars, the beat of their drums, and their shouts and songs resounding through the forest, scaring the langurs, and perhaps making the Bengali villagers a little jealous of their capacity for uninhibited, unrestricted enjoyment.

Epilogue

Exiles

It was too late to travel further west and north; my visa had less than two days to run and if I failed to get a seat on the plane to Calcutta I'd have to leave by road, by the same route we'd come in – which would take more than two days.

Fortunately someone cancelled their ticket at the last minute, and with a few hours of my visa to run I found myself on a plane, sitting next to a high caste Hindu, a Brahmin from West Bengal. He was a businessman and politely asked what I'd been doing in Bangladesh. Relieved of the need to lie I told him; he wasn't really interested, although he found it extraordinary that I'd been travelling the rural areas voluntarily by bus ('so uncomfortable'), by boat ('so dirty'), and even on foot (words failed him).

His ancient Aryan prejudices began to well up at the mention of Mru, Khasi and Mandi – not surprisingly, as the first Aryan settlers in the subcontinent characterized the tribal people as devils. One poet opened his account of a tribal army with a list of unflattering, if imaginative similes: 'A crowd of evil deeds come together', and 'A caravan of curses', while the *Mahabharata* classes them with the sinful creatures of the earth.

I insisted that I found such people congenial company, but he didn't believe me, and we didn't understand each other. I was glad when the plane touched down at Dum Dum airport forty minutes after take-off.

The person I really wanted to see was Bimal Bhikkhu, and in a few days Mukta would be joining me in Calcutta.

India was building up to its Assembly elections – the walls were covered in political graffiti – and the talk was of war in Kashmir, with Pakistan. The headlines blared at passers-by on Chowringhee: 'War Games'. They asked 'Is War Inevitable?', and carried photographs of burning buildings, soldiers and frightened citizenry. Beside all this a report in one paper that ten thousand more tribal people from the Chittagong Hill Tracts had been evicted and were moving towards the Indian border went almost unnoticed.

The streets around the Bengal Buddhist Temple, in central Calcutta, are residential: red brick government flats with green Venetian shutters and grilles. The population is mixed: Bengalis, Chinese and Eurasians live together in relative harmony. The narrow side street where the temple lies had been blocked off for a game of cricket earlier in the day, and when I arrived the local team was celebrating its victory with speeches and a barrage of fire crackers.

Two hundred yards away, but hidden by high buildings, runs Chitaranjan Avenue, where buses, cars and taxis churn up dust and pour carbon dioxide into the already loaded air. Trams make their rumbling, careful way through the chaos with a discreet 'ting-ting', which is somehow audible above all the other noise.

The temple complex itself was no ocean of calm: gangs of chattering school girls filled the courtyard, and an added cause for excitement was the presence of four visiting Korean monks, armed with a video camera. The temple school dance class was going to perform a dramatized version of the Buddha's life, in the visitors' honour. Preparations were in full swing, and to add to the confusion a family of Tibetans from Darjeeling, loaded down with tin trunks, bedding rolls and suitcases, were on their way through. They were on a winter pilgrimage to Bodh Gaya, where the Buddha gained enlightenment. Their children ran around like little savages, dirty and naughty, afraid of nothing, except perhaps their grandmother who presided over the group like the matriarch she was. She ordered her mincing, stretch-jean and T-shirt clad daughters-in-law about with the confidence of long command.

The main temple building was constructed a hundred years ago, and is painted a shocking pink. The monks live in rooms above the shrine, reached via a rusty spiral staircase, and it was there that I found Bimal. He'd just returned from Japan, the biggest aid donor to Bangladesh, where he'd been trying to persuade the Japanese government to reduce its aid commitment until the human rights' situation in the Hill Tracts improves. He laughed happily as he told me what happened when he called a press conference. 'Before the conference the Bangladesh Embassy in Tokyo issued a statement saying that I wasn't a Bangladeshi, and urged journalists not to come because everything I say is a lie. But of course that only made the journalists more interested to find out what the fuss was about. So the Embassy actually had the opposite effect to what it wanted. I was even on Japanese TV!'

There isn't much likelihood of Tokyo reducing aid to Bangladesh, or making it dependent on an improved human rights' record, but the issue had been enthusiastically taken up, Bimal said, by Buddhist groups there.

He was tired of all the travelling he has to do, and of his busy life. 'I'd like to give it up for a hut under a tree by a river. My only possession would be an alms bowl, I could do it you know, I could live like that.'

'I'm sure you could, Bimal,' I said, but couldn't help teasing him by adding that people would soon find him out, and come demanding to be told the Way, or the Truth, and that then his life would be as busy as it is now.

'Oh, I'd send them away,' he said stubbornly, 'tell them that I know nothing.'

In reality he won't give up his human rights' work, he can't; too many of his friends and acquaintances have been killed. In 1986 one of the schools which he ran for tribal children orphaned by the war in the Hill Tracts was torched by a gang of Bengali settlers, protected by the Bangladesh army. Of the three hundred odd children only a hundred and fifty managed to escape through the jungle to Tripura in India – a three-day journey made more difficult by the necessity of avoiding army patrols. Fifty found their way to friends or relatives, but the whereabouts of the remaining hundred children is still unknown. Shortly after this event Bimal himself was forced to flee Bangladesh, when the government started to assassinate tribal intellectuals and monks. Now, apart from his human rights' work, he tries to help the sixty-five thousand refugees from the Hill Tracts, ten per cent of the total tribal population, living in appalling conditions in refugee camps in India. No one else helps them, not the United Nations' High Commission for Refugees, the Red Cross, Oxfam, Save the Children, or any of the international agencies which are supposed to do this work.

Bimal wanted me to meet some of the young, educated Chakma driven away by fear. They too were refugees and had terrible stories to tell of murder, rape and torture, and their friends in jail. One young man, hardly more than a boy, had been lined up with the rest of his village by an army major, perhaps the same urbane major who'd let Peter and myself off so lightly. One by one the whole village was interrogated on the whereabouts of the Shanti Bahini, the tribal guerrilla army. No one knew anything, but the major decided to make an example of this boy.

He called a soldier and ordered him to shoot the teenager in the knee. Then they took him to hospital, where the same major ordered a doctor to amputate the injured leg. The doctor pointed out that the limb could be saved, and then did what the major wanted.

And Bimal told me more, saying that now the majority of the tribal people in the Hill Tracts are destitute. 'It's not too bad in the south yet, where you went, but elsewhere they've lost their land, they can't get jobs, and they're not allowed to work. The government herds them into cluster villages, and sometimes gives food, clothes, whatever. In that sense the government has been successful; if people don't do what the army says they die. It's that simple. The government doesn't need to kill people with guns any more. The latest plan is for the cluster villages to be given aid projects – growing mushrooms, producing handicrafts, that kind of thing – to show that the government is looking after the welfare of my people. But if it wasn't for the government they wouldn't need any of these things.'

He speaks with so little rancour that it's hard to believe he's talking about the destruction of a whole people – their way of life, their culture, their lives – and harder still to believe that they're his people. It's not that he speaks quietly, but rather in a level tone – perhaps Buddhism has taught him how to control his emotions, or perhaps he's learnt that such statements have more force on the world's stage, in the UN and in government offices in a dozen different capitals, if they're uttered dispassionately.

I asked him how he squared the Buddhist belief that the world and its pain is an illusion with his political involvement. He didn't like the word 'political', adding that philosophy wasn't his subject, but he said, 'Although pain is an illusion, it doesn't mean there's nothing there. Maybe we misinterpret the signs. A rope, for instance, can easily be mistaken for a snake at night. Both pain and pleasure exist in the mind alone, but I still believe that it's important to do something for those who are unable to understand this.

'The world is full of greed for power and for material goods. Some people want to be superior, and the only way they can be is by taking power. That's what's happening in the Hill Tracts. Oppression is only another form of greed, which results in the violation of human rights. People who aren't greedy for power and possessions find it hard to protect themselves against those who are. So it's necessary to help them.'

He smiled broadly, as though he'd struggled through an exam – the concepts must be difficult in a foreign language. 'I'm sorry that I can't explain it better. If you want to know more you should ask someone else, someone who knows more Buddhist philosophy. But I want to ask whether you achieved what you set out to do by travelling the border?'

I tried to avoid answering the question, not knowing the answer. 'I didn't set out to achieve anything, and anyway isn't achievement a very un-Buddhist idea?'

He laughed, 'OK, I'll put it another way. What did you learn?'

'If you ask again tomorrow I'll try and tell you.'

That evening I went back to the thick exercise book in which I'd made notes of our v-shaped journey, down the coast, to St Martin's Island, and then inland and north. I read through my descriptions and observations, and thought of how the two cultural blocks, plain and hill, were acting like grinding stones on the people between them. That in turn made me think of the manner in which the Chakma, the Mru, and the Mandi are being pushed from the plains, and I grew bitter. The to-and-fro battle along the border has been going on for centuries, but there's still no excuse for the cruelties or for the greed, as Bimal put it. The difference is that now the thirteen tribal nations of the Chittagong Hill Tracts are facing extinction; their choice is between losing everything and being forcibly absorbed into mainstream Bangladeshi society, or becoming refugees, stateless and powerless, and fighting, however hopeless their cause may seem. Unlike the Mandi or the Khasi, or the Manipuri, they don't have larger communities across the border in India – the Chittagong Hill Tracts is their land.

It was after midnight, and Buddhist Temple Street had been quiet for at least an hour, so it was all the more startling when a woman started shouting in front of the government flats. A neighbour had insulted her in some way, and now, when everyone could hear, she was having her revenge. She heaped insult on insult, occasionally stopping to regain her breath or think up stronger terms of abuse, and she was allowed to continue for an hour before her mother, or her sister, came out and led her inside, still shouting.

I went back even further, to the notes I'd made months before, sitting in the sunless library of the School of Oriental and African Studies in London. There were dates and names, and quotations from luminaries as far apart as Dr Samuel Johnson ('What a wretch that must be who is content with such conversation as can be had among savages!'), and Sayyid Ahmadi ('Islam and idolatory are as mixed as kedgeree in Bengal'). It was late. These and other quotations seemed to say more about the writers themselves, their ideas and concerns, than about either Bengalis or tribal people. I felt more confused and less likely to come up with an answer to Bimal's question than when he had put it to me.

It began to rain, the drops falling solidly through the city's humid, polluted air and into the dust of the road outside my window. I thought back to when I'd been planning the journey, and how this was to be my last trip to Bangladesh, how I believed that I'd written myself dry on the subject. As I watched the water rise, drowning the road, I realized that even this time I'd barely touched the people of the edge: *hijra*, prostitutes, peasants, *pir*, beggars, Bedeh, Rakhine, Chakma, Mru, Manipuri, Khasi, and Mandi. And I knew that I wanted to, that I will return to walk the hills and jungles of the Chittagong Hill Tracts again; to get to know the girl prostitute, Leila; the *hijra*, Nargis; to cross the northern marshland with the wild people who inhabit the place; and to enjoy once again the hospitality of the Manipuri and the Mandi.

In reality I may never get the chance – it seems unlikely that the Bangladesh government will welcome me back – but my interest in and enthusiasm for the northeastern tribal states has been whetted still further; perhaps one day the Indian government will issue that Special Permit, and I'll be able to meet the tribal peoples on their own ground, where they're in the majority, and where they feel relatively secure.

It was my last night in Calcutta, and the next morning Bimal had to be content with this slight explanation and this hope for the future, because when Mukta arrived at midday we were going down the coast together, to the Black Pagoda at Konarak, to Madras, to the great temple complex at Madurai, until we reached a quiet beach in the south, where all the old myths might come true.